VICAR'S WORLD

Bill Ritson &
Patrick Forbes

Other titles in the Humour Series available from Jarrold Colour Publications.

Whine and Dine by Lesley and Cris de Boos

Westminster Exposed by Ian Collins

Racey Bits by Mark Siggers and Chris Williams

Vicar's World

ISBN 0-7117-0353-1
First published in Great Britain, 1988

Designed and produced by Parke Sutton Limited, 8 Thorpe Road, Norwich NR1 1RY for Jarrold Colour Publications, Barrack Street, Norwich NR3 1TR. Printed in England.

About the Authors

Patrick Forbes

Advised by her doctor not to have the child, his mother disagreed and had him induced early to meet a copy date. In 1947 she wished she'd taken the doctor's advice, and shipped him off to boarding school in Eastbourne.

After 'O' levels he trained as Merchant Navy Radio Officer and travelled widely before coming ashore to marry. Gainful employment then included moving furniture, servicing telephone answering machines, and working as a technical engineer in a recording studio.

He trained at Lincoln Theological College and, ordained in 1966, served as a curate at Yeovil then worked at Thamesmead in South London for nine years where he had particular responsibility for community development before his appointment in 1978 as Communications Officer for St Albans Diocese.

He researched *Priestland's Progress* and *The Case Against God* for BBC Radio 4, and has been working in local radio since 1981. He believes in God, marriage, love and laughter and has written a book, *The Gospel of Folly.*

Bill Ritson

Bill Ritson was born in Sunderland in 1935, the year which also witnessed the birth of Elvis Presley, Lester Piggott and Penguin Books. He was baptised Gerald Richard Stanley (after his father and two grandfathers), but as soon as his parents got outside the church they called him 'Bill'.

He was educated at Durham School where he acted in plays, and at Corpus Christi College, Cambridge, where he turned his attention to revues and cabaret.

After two years at Lincoln Theological College he was ordained at St Albans Cathedral in 1961. Since then, he has served in two parishes in Hertfordshire and two in Bedfordshire, and has also been Chaplain to the Bishop. He is now a Residentiary Canon of St Albans.

Bill is unmarried, but has eleven God-children, three nephews, two lodgers and a teddy bear called Bunbury.

Introduction

A holy man once said, 'To believe, you have to laugh ... to laugh, you have to believe.' Ever since there has been faith or belief, there has been laughter and there have been religious jokes – whether about bishops and actresses, clergy falling into graves, or rabbis being misspelt as rabbits.

This book takes a sideways look at religion as we find it. We meet saints, sinners, priests and the occasional prostitute. We discover things even we didn't know about religion, the church, the faith. Here are stories about baptisms, weddings, funerals – the hatches, matches and dispatches of church life. There are potted biographies of people you've never heard of – Rahab, for example, to say nothing of St Serge of Crampolinas, the first priest to fly.

You'll find explanations for almost everything, and where we can't explain, as happens sometimes, we attempt to describe what we see. Once you've mastered even a quarter of the contents of the book, you should be able to hold your own in any theological college, any manse, presbytery, vicarage or rectory.

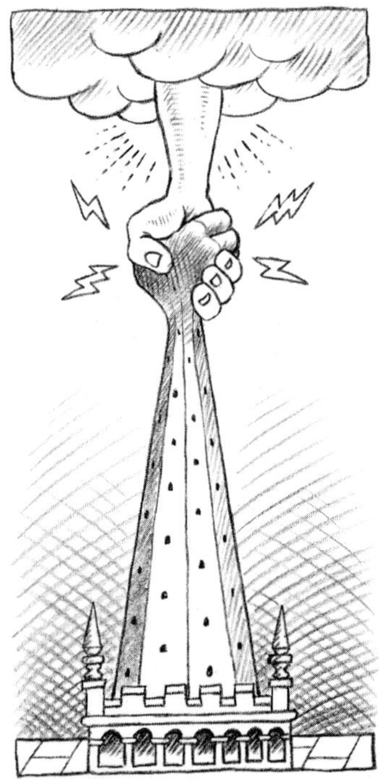

Abbot

Not only a popular brewed ale, but also the superior of a large religious house such as a monastery. The word comes from the Syriac word *abba,* meaning father. Within the Benedictine community, the abbot is elected for life by members of the community, and exercises authority over his brothers. In the Middle Ages, an Abbot of Misrule was appointed to preside over Christmas revels, a celebration linked with the Feast of Fools. Alexander Pope in the *The Dunciad* talks of:

Happy Convents, bosomed deep in vines,
Where slumber abbots, purple as their wines.

Absalom

Son of David in Old Testament. He rode a mule under thick boughs of a great oak, his head caught fast in the branches and he was left hanging. An old edition of the Bible in verse describes the incident:

Among the boughs the rebel there
Was left suspended by the hair.

This charming rhyme is accompanied by a hair-raising picture of the unfortunate Absalom hanging from the tree as his mule galloped away.

Acolyte

Not a form of fire-lighter, but an attendant at church who usually carries a lighted candle in procession.

Alexandria, St Catherine of

Back in Egypt, about 16 centuries ago, Catherine was tied to a wheel set with knives and spikes and other nasties, in order to bring her to a most uncomfortable death. But the spikes *et al* flew off and impaled her persecutors instead. And very right too. Since then she's become the patron saint of fireworks manufacturers – or more possibly of their accountants.

Amen and Alleluia

Amen and *Alleluia* are two Hebrew words which are never translated into any other language. *Amen* means 'So be it' and in times of war people can be heard praying for 'our men. Amen.' *Alleluia* is a cry of praise, and a favourite word among the kind of Christians who cannot resist shouting out in the middle of worship. They are also apt to wave their arms in the air.

Andrew, St

The brother of Peter – and the patron saint of Scotland, where a city is named after him. The cathedrals of Rochester and Wells are dedicated to him, and he is remembered on 30 November. Represented in numerous paintings and carvings with his 'X'-shaped cross or 'saltire' upon which, it is said, he was crucified. That same saltire is also Scotland's part of the Union Flag.

A Angels

Angels

Not to be confused with freshly scrubbed choirboys in white surplices, angels are to be found throughout the Old and New Testaments of the Bible. The word is derived from the Greek word meaning a messenger. In St Luke's story of the nativity, the Archangel Gabriel tells Mary she is to have a baby, an angel appears to the shepherds near Bethlehem, and the skies fill with angels praising God. When they're not delivering messages, angels spend their time lauding The Almighty – which is very right and proper.

Anglicans

Not just the Church of England, but members of a world-wide Church with 'branches' in 164 countries and a global membership estimated at around 70 million. Within this total are 27 self-governing churches subdivided into more than 400 dioceses, 30,000 parishes and over 60,000 individual congregations.

Fragmentary as it is, it still has an amazingly enduring strength. The Anglican Church throughout the world is like a very large family with a rich tradition of mutual affection and support. Like any family it has its disagreements, but its strengths are far greater than its differences.

Time was when the Church of England was called 'the Tory party at prayer'. Recent debates on the bomb and the inner cities, and criticism by bishops of government policies demonstrate that this could hardly be said to be the case now.

Archdeacon

An archdeacon is the bishop's right hand man. He travels round the diocese inspecting drains and gutters. 'Arch' in this context actually means chief or pre-eminent, and 'deacon' means minister or servant.

He is known by the title 'Venerable', but the most famous person to be honoured with such a title, the Venerable Bede, was not an archdeacon.

Ark

One of the best cartoons is a picture of Noah's ark, with Noah and his family scratching themselves and hitting out with fly swats. The animals crowded on board look faintly puzzled. Noah is saying to his family, 'I think we should have drawn the line at fruit flies.'

Repeated attempts to find Noah's ark have failed, though the slopes of Mount Ararat in eastern Turkey have been combed by excited archaeologists.

Noah's ark is not to be confused with the Ark of the Covenant, a holy box which contained the ten commandments written on stone.

ASB (Alternative Service Book)

This new prayer book, published in 1980, is the first authorised alternative to the Book of Common Prayer (BCP) which dates from 1662. It caused a storm of criticism and controversy when it was published – but with the passing of time most people (diehards excepted) are getting used to it. It is intended to be a complement to the BCP. Many churches have both and use them on different occasions, the decision to use or not to use being left to the discretion of individual parochial church councils.

Couples being married may be glad to be able to choose an alternative to the 1662 introduction to the marriage service which speaks of 'satisfying men's carnal lusts and appetites, like brute beasts having no understanding.'

Ashes

Ashes in the church today are usually the remains of a human body, or the remains of palm crosses. However, in days of old, they were more likely to be connected with the boiler or stove used for the heating of the place. These monstrous contraptions used to rumble menacingly in the background throughout services, and on occasion shower unwelcome ashes over the congregation.

Nowadays, in complete contrast, on Ash Wednesday – the First Day of Lent – some congregations actually come to church with the express desire of having ashes rubbed on their foreheads. These ashes, made from the previous year's burnt palm crosses, are placed in a bowl into which the priest dips his finger before tracing the sign of the cross on the worshipper's brow – an ancient custom which dates from earlier, more gutsy days when penitents appeared clothed in sackcloth before the bishop, who sprinkled ashes over their heads. This symbol of penitence owes its origin to the biblical reminder that 'for dust thou art, and unto dust thou shall return'.

Cremated ashes may be buried in the churchyard, but the church plays no part in scattering them.

Baptism

Also known as Christening, this is the rite of entry into membership of the Church.

In warm climes the candidates may be asked to wade out into the midst of the local river where the minister, clad in baptismal waders, will push them under the water and duck them three times (the traditional number of sinkings before one drowns) in the name of the Father, the Son and Holy Spirit, but allow them to emerge before they finally expire.

In colder countries, Baptism is more usually of infants upon whose head the priest sprinkles water, or pours it from a shell. This water is usually warmed beforehand to prevent the baby dying of shock. Many babies, however, register their total disapproval in the loudest possible manner. These children insist on taking a lively part in the ceremony themselves by competing with the priest to see who can shout the loudest. The priest, like all adults, always has the last word by splashing the water with gay abandon all over the protesting infant's face.

The story is told of a very stern and strict, grim and frowning priest who at one baptism demanded of the terrified parents holding their baby girl, 'Name this child!'

'Lucy sir,' replied the trembling mother.

'Lucifer! I refuse to name any child Lucifer!' cried the priest and, dipping his finger in the water before sprinkling the baby's forehead, he declared, 'I name thee John.'

Other unfortunate children have been christened with 12 names after the players of an entire football team – or, perhaps worst, after the full line-up of a pop group.

Baptists

Baptists, a very individual congregation, are dissenters. A Baptist minister in London, on the occasion of the death of Queen Anne, is said to have preached on the text, 'Go find the harlot and bury her, for she is a queen.' The queen in the text was Jezebel, who died a hideous death.

The dissent of the Baptists arises from their belief about the nature of the Church, which they see as a community of believers rather than a massive institution. Baptism, therefore, is a sign of conscious belief by an adult.

A young Baptist minister graphically described his anxieties at one of the first total-immersion baptisms at which he officiated. 'There was this lady,' he said, 'You know, the sort who kick-starts jumbo jets . . . How was I to get her to stand up after her baptism?' His was not a totally buoyant faith, it seemed.

Fellowship is a buzzword among Baptists. One preacher who had travelled all the way from Oxford to a Norfolk church reported, 'Instead of being asked what travelling costs I had incurred, this man said, "Brother, may we have fellowship in the petrol?" '

Bartholomew, St

One of the 12 disciples about whom little is known. Matthew, Mark and Luke call him Bartholomew, but John considers that too difficult and names him Nathanael instead. His emblem is a butcher's flaying knife – with which, so tradition has it, he was martyred rather nastily somewhere along the Caspian Sea. His persecutors first of all flayed him alive – which is presumably why he is the patron saint of tanners. More peaceably, one of the great London hospitals carries his name.

Benedictine

A liqueur, quite delicious, offered to guests on feast days at Benedictine Abbeys where the monks follow the rule of St Benedict.

Of ancient origin, the liqueur is produced at Fécamp in Normandy and is a distillate which has been flavoured with more than 20 herbs, aged and blended, then coloured dark amber by the addition of caramel and a little saffron. The 'DOM' on every bottle label is the initials of the Benedictine maxim – *Deo Optimo, Maximo:* To God, most good, most high.

The Benedictine order was founded in AD 529. English Benedictine houses include Ampleforth in Yorkshire where Cardinal Hume was once Abbot, Douai in Berkshire and Buckfast in Devon.

Kipling speaks of Brandy for the Parson; and in the Bible there is much talk of spirits, some being more acceptable than others. There is a mention of putting down the bier at Nain, and of watering the wine at Cana where the best was kept until last.

Benjamin

The leading character played by Dustin Hoffman in the 1960s film *The Graduate* who, to the music of Simon and Garfunkel, was greatly surprised by Mrs Robinson, portrayed by Anne Bancroft.

In the Old Testament, Benjamin was the youngest son of Jacob – whose own sons were equally happy to surprise the Virgins of Shiloh in the last chapter of the Book of Judges, catching them as they danced.

Bible

The Breeches Bible is so called because, where the Authorised Version of 1611 has aprons as the clothes made by Adam and Eve out of fig leaves, the Geneva Bible published in 1560 offers breeches.

In 1641 a printer made a serious error by omitting the ward 'not' from the prohibition on adultery in Exodus Chapter 20, verse 14. The printer was fined £300, a heavy fine in those days.

When asked to swear an oath on the Bible, it's worth remembering the words from the Sermon on the Mount where Jesus advises his listeners not to swear at all but, 'Let your communication be Yea, yea; Nay, nay; for whatsoever is more than these cometh of evil.'

They like to tell you (or used to, in more peaceable days) in the picturesque little port of Byblos, in North Lebanon, that their town gave its name to the Bible. Not so, unfortunately: it's derived from the Greek *Ta Biblia* through medieval Latin, and means 'the books'.

The all-time best seller, it is worth noting that by 1965 the Bible had been circulated by the United Bible Societies in a staggering total of 1,251 languages.

Biretta

Not the small automatic weapon carried by secret agents in James Bond films. That's a beretta.

A biretta is a less dangerous accessory and is a square-shaped hat worn by clergy for some of the time and Chesterton's Father Brown all of the time. Once upon a time it was worn by senior graduates at university. Like cassocks, birettas are helpfully colour-coded: black for the common-or-garden clergy, purple for bishops, red for cardinals and white, not for the Pope, but for Premonstratensian canons, whatever they are, and Cistercian abbots.

Bishop

The butt of jokes about actresses, and often a figure of fun in comedy series such as *All Gas and Gaiters,* the bishop has a central role in many churches. The word comes from the Greek word for overseer – someone who oversees an area and, more importantly, people.

Depending on his seniority he may be required to take one of the 21 seats reserved for bishops in the House of Lords. The two Archbishops – and the Bishops of London, Winchester and Durham – are members of the House by virtue of their appointments. The Bishop of Bath and Wells lives in a moated palace, where hungry swans ring a bell at meal times. When bishops sign documents, they substitute the Roman or English name of their diocese for their surname: thus John St Albans, William Petriburg, Fred Bath et Well, Harry Sodor and Man.

Bishops carry a pastoral staff or crook symbolising their role as shepherd of the flock, and wear mitres. Their shirts, and sometimes their socks, are purple. They wear a pectoral cross on a chain round the neck, and an episcopal ring, often on the third finger of the right hand. The choice of finger on which a bishop wears the ring which signals his authority is not strictly laid down – we are assured (by a Bishop, no less) that the ring finger is optional!

Boat Boy

Not the guardian of the Bishop's Barge, but the boy or man in charge of the incense.

The boat boy carries the censer in which incense is placed over hot charcoal to produce, on demand, the aromatic smoke symbolising prayer and the presence of God in worship.

It is his responsibility to have the incense prepared and ready for the priest who will cense the altar, the people, and the Bible before the Gospel is read.

Book of Kells

A beautifully-decorated manuscript of the Gospels from the monastery of Kells in Ireland, dating from the 8th century. Similar to the Lindisfarne Gospels of the same era. The Lindisfarne Gospels are kept in the British Museum in the same room as Magna Carta and the original manuscript of *Yesterday* by Paul McCartney.

Bray, Vicar of

The Vicar of Bray, celebrated in a song written in the early 18th century, was a priest who managed to keep his head under both Charles II and George I. Whatever doctrine was the fashion, he would follow it. His one abiding aim in life, enshrined in a traditional English song, was that 'Whatsoever King shall reign, I will be the Vicar of Bray, Sir!'

No-one has been able to establish the identity of this Berkshire vicar, testimony to his ability to trim his beliefs to suit the climate of the day and hide his identity. There's a limerick which runs:

An indolent Vicar of Bray,
Allowed his flowers to decay.
His wife, more alert,
Bought a powerful squirt,
And said to her spouse, 'Let us spray.'

Burial

Burial is the reverent laying-to-rest of a dead body in the earth. 'The Burial of the Dead' is the Prayer Book title for a funeral service, and 'burial ground' is a name for a cemetery.

The first words of the Anglican Burial Service are 'I am the Resurrection and the Life, says the Lord' and it is one of a priest's nightmares that he will one day (mistakenly) launch into this at the start of a wedding as he gazes at the happy couple. This is not such an unlikely scenario, as the same hymn – 'The Lord's my Shepherd', sung to the tume *Crimond* – is in the top ten for both funerals and weddings.

The story is told of a man whose dog brought into the house the body of his next door neighbour's dead rabbit.

'Oh Lord,' thought the man. 'What will they say? Rover must have killed it.'

He was so anxious not to upset his neighbour that he took the corpse and spruced it up as much as he could. He washed the fur a bit and blow-dried it, brushed it and fluffed it up, then took the body and laid it, all bright and clean and white, just over the hedge in the neighbour's garden.

Not long after, round came the neighbour, fearfully agitated and alarmed.

'Oh my God,' he said. 'What in the world can have happened? Bunny died yesterday and I buried him in the garden – but come over here and just look at him now!'

Death does not take the old but the ripe.
Russian proverb

Caesarea

Ancient biblical town, sited in modern Israel on the Mediterranean coast between Tel Aviv and Haifa. Originally built by Herod the Great, it had a large early Christian community and was for a time the capital of Roman Palestine. Its modern lot is to be an archaeological dig and a tourist resort.

Not to be confused with an inquiry as to the whereabouts of the Roman Emperor, as in 'Is Caesarea?'

Cain and Abel

Not the leading characters in a novel by Jeffrey Archer, but two brothers in the book of Genesis, one of whom killed the other. Abel was not able to escape. It was Cain who killed, slaying his brother, according to tradition, with the jaw-bone of an ass. Cain was later to be cut down by an arrow, when a hunter mistook him for a wild beast . . .

Campanology

Campanology (or bell-ringing) is a very serious business requiring great concentration and the most precise timing – but, as the noise from many a rural belfry will confirm, not always getting it.

Ringers usually climb up to a chamber in the tower where they stand in a circle and pull coloured ropes called sallies, while their leader utters little ritual cries. They ring for about half an hour before worship, and then, as the service begins, the opening words of the minister are likely to be punctuated by the sound of the boots of the ringers

descending the steps and making a hasty exit from the building . . . generally in the direction of the local pub.

The most famous bellringer of all was probably Quasimodo of Notre Dame.

Candlemas

The feast of the Purification of the Blessed Virgin Mary and the Presentation of Christ in the Temple, usually celebrated on 2 February when candles are blessed and carried in procession.

According to the Laws of Moses set out in the Old Testament, a mother was unclean after the birth of a male child and disqualified from touching any hallowed thing for 40 days, at the end of which time she went to the Temple with an offering and was purified.

So the Virgin Mary, at the appointed time, went to the Temple with Joseph and the Christ Child.

Within living memory, such 'churching' of women by the priest, usually in the church porch, was an accepted tradition in rural England.

In the United States, 2 February is National Groundhog Day when the groundhogs peer out after their winter hibernation. If it is a dull rainy day they come out, for that means that winter is over. But if it is sunny, they go to sleep again because that means the weather will be cold and wintry for another six weeks or so. And there's an old English countryman's rhyme that comes to a similar conclusion:

If Candlemas Day be fair and bright,
Winter will take another flight.
If Candlemas Day be cloudy and rain
Winter is gone and will not come again.

Don't curse the darkness – light a candle.
Chinese proverb

Canon

One of the big guns of the Church.

Canons have special seats in cathedrals known as 'stalls'. Most cathedrals have about four Residentiary Canons who are on the permanent staff and help the Dean (the vicar of a cathedral) to run the place. There are also about 20 Honorary Canons who also have stalls, but come to the cathedral only on big occasions. Honorary Canons usually have parishes of their own where they live and work, but they are given the honorary title of 'Canon' as a reward for faithful service.

Just to be confusing, the Canons of the Church of England are also Ecclesiastical Laws. And, inevitably, there have been lawyer Canons administering Canon Law.

A coven of Canons is known as a Chapter, but 'to canonise' someone means not to make him a Canon, but to make him a Saint. Few Canons have actually been canonised, and, it's good to report, few Canons have ever actually been fired.

I have, alas, only one illusion left,
and that is the Archbishop of Canterbury.
Sydney Smith

CANTERBURY

Before travel agents discovered the Costa Brava or Luton Airport, people trekked to Canterbury on pilgrimage. Medieval package tours included overnight stops at watering holes like Croydon, spare sandals and all the ale you could sink along the Pilgrim's Way. To get the true flavour of the pilgrimage, read Chaucer's *Canterbury Tales.*

The pilgrimage always took place at the same time, in spring each year . . .'Whan that Aprille with his shoures sote/The droghte of Marche hath perced to the rote' – and was taken up, in Chaucer's wonderfully lively, earthy version, with story-telling to lighten the long hours *en route.*

One of the earliest foreign missionaries to try to convert the Anglo Saxons to Christianity was Saint Augustine who arrived in Canterbury in 597. Thomas à Becket was murdered in the city's cathedral by knights acting for King Henry on 29 December, 1170. The King, protesting that it was all a dreadful mistake, later came and did public penance for the crime.

The Archbishop of Canterbury is both bishop of the diocese of Canterbury, where he has a palace, and Primate of the Church of England with his headquarters at Lambeth.

CAROL

A song sung in and out of churches to mark Christmas, Advent or Easter. The word comes from the Italian word *carola,* meaning a ring dance, and so the word meant 'dance' before it meant a song.

The best collection of carols is probably *The Oxford Book of Carols,* and the best carol singing traditionally comes from King's College, Cambridge, where the Festival of Nine Lessons and Carols is held and broadcast each year.

The tradition of carol singing from door to door was certainly pre-Victorian and those who sang were called Waits. Originally in medieval England Waits were watchmen, who marked the hours of the night by sounding musical instruments. Later they became the official 'town bands', turning out to support the mayor on special occasions. The city of York reformed their Waits band some years ago; the city of Norwich followed suit in 1986. So much for the pleasant thought that the word indicated, during those carol-singing promenades, a long wait on the doorstep before the occupant opens up, curses the noise, hands out money or, best of all, invites the Waits in for hot punch and mince pies.

CARROLL, LEWIS

Pen name of the Reverend Charles Lutwidge Dodgson, Victorian priest, mathematician, author and artist.

The son of a clergyman and the oldest of eleven children, Dodgson was born on 27 January 1832. He had a curious childhood, remarkable for arming insects with swords and making them fight one another.

Unhappy at Rugby School, he went up to Oxford in 1851 where, after graduating, he joined the Mathematics Faculty, writing papers on geometry and logic. It was at Oxford that Dodgson first told the stories of *Alice in Wonderland* and *Through the Looking Glass* to the daughter of the Dean of his college. Among his other works are *Jabberwocky, Phantasmagoria,* and *The Hunting of the Snark*. He was a pioneer photographer, and wrote *Hiawatha's Photographing,* a parody of Longfellow's *Hiawatha.*

Ordained deacon in 1861, Dodgson died at Guildford on 14 January 1898, never having married.

One of the Church's favourite Carrolls. . . ?

CASSOCK

A long dress-like garment, usually black, worn by clergy. The word – quite logically, judging from the appearance of the garment – comes from the Italian, *casacca,* an overcoat. It dates from around the 6th century when pagan hemlines rose, and clergy hemlines stayed firmly near the ground – presumably so you could tell heathen and clergy apart!

It's a marvellous garment for concealing all manner of unfashionable, outdated or inappropriate clothing, never mind anything else. Theological students – pathologically incapable of arriving in College on time – throw on their cassocks over pyjamas, or underwear or (perish the thought) nothing at all. The practice leads to breathless prayers for clement weather with an absence of high winds or inquisitive ladies.

Cassocks in Western Christianity are helpfully colour-coded to assist the innocent abroad and at home. Black is safe, for the occupant is a run of the mill clergyperson. Women, too, wear cassocks. A purple cassock proclaims there's a bishop inside. Red, a warning colour, betokens a cardinal within. If you see a white cassock, it's got to be the Pope, so hit the ground FAST!

The only other thing to say about cassocks is that they're a gift to writers of religious limericks . . . what else rhymes with hassocks?

Cathedral

The principal church of a diocese where the Bishop has his *cathedra*, his seat or throne. A cathedral is run by the Dean or Provost, and a Chapter of Canons or Prebendaries.

Some cathedrals are very long – like Winchester and St Albans; some are small like St David's, Dyfed; some are on the top of a hill like Durham and Lincoln; some with a spire like Salisbury and Norwich; some with a dome like St Paul's. But each is the mother church of its diocese, and many contain the shrines of saints, the cathedrals at St Albans and St David's being obvious examples. But not all cathedrals take a saint's name for their own, even though there are some close associations: St Cuthbert is remembered at Durham, St Chad at Lichfield, St Richard at Chichester and St Hugh at Lincoln, to name but a few.

Nearly all cathedrals have choirs and a strong musical tradition. Another tradition is that these choirs are exclusively male.

Nowadays, cathedrals are great tourist attractions, but they are not just ancient monuments. Many of them house works by famous 20th-century artists: Chichester, for instance, has beautiful pieces by John Piper, Graham Sutherland and Marc Chagall.

Chancel

The part of a church east of the nave, usually comprising the sanctuary. In some churches, the chancel is separated from the nave by a screen fashioned from stone, wood or metal.

Before Henry VIII's time, the chancel was restricted to the clergy and the celebration of the Mass, the people occupying only the nave. Separating them was the screen, or lattice (the Latin for which, *cancelli*, is the origin of the word 'chancel'). There are sometimes steps leading up to the chancel from the nave. Not surprisingly, these are often called chancel steps, and are handy for bride and groom to use for kneeling during the marriage ceremony. The step also makes it easier to rise from the kneeling position.

A bridegroom once knelt at the chancel step, and from the congregation came a barely suppressed tittering. Some 'friend' had lettered the soles of his shoes in large white letters, HE on the left sole, and LP on the right.

Chantry

Villains, wife-beaters or barons afflicted with a conscience about ill-treating their subjects, might suddenly ask a priest to say prayers for their soul after they've died (leaving a large bequest in their Wills to pay for it) in the hope that such prayers might help them get to heaven rather than the other place. A chantry was a chapel for this purpose.

Usually they were built within a church, screened off from the main worship area, but sometimes in the churchyard and occasionally on bridges.

The catch, of course, was that there was no guarantee that the prayers and Masses – which had to be paid for – would achieve the desired effect. But then, in the Middle Ages, hardly anything was certain.

Chapel of Ease

Not a pushover for idle curates, but a chapel built in areas where people might find it difficult to travel to the mother church of the parish or district. They do not generally have their own priest in charge; neither are they equipped with deck-chairs or cold-drinks dispensers.

Chaplain

An ecclesiastical title often used to describe a priest ministering in some specialised area. There are school chaplains, hospital chaplains, industrial chaplains and prison chaplains, to name but a few. In the Army, Royal Navy and RAF the chaplains to the various services take various services.

Some years ago when the post of Chaplain to Durham School fell vacant, a delightful advertisement appeared asking for applications for a 'Chaplin'. Whoever printed that must have felt a right Charlie.

Chaplains to the Queen do not like to draw attention to themselves, and therefore wear bright red cassocks when all their colleagues are in black. On one occasion, when dining in a distinguished London club with one of these exotic creatures, one member of the party quietly announced to a third person at the table that, 'Canon So-and-So is a Chaplain to the Queen.'

'Ssh', whispered the aforesaid Canon modestly. 'I do not like to draw attention to the fact that I AM CHAPLAIN TO THE QUEEN!' His voice rose to a crescendo as he roared out the last seven words. The other diners, naturally, took not the slightest notice as they were either deaf or too polite or both, and the Canon's desire for privacy was in no way impaired.

Trust in God but mind your business.
Russian proverb

Chapter

Collection of Canons. In olden days the Canons used to meet in the Chapter House to hear a chapter of the Bible or some Holy Book; hence the name.

Nowadays, one could write a whole book, chapter upon chapter, about the goings-on among the Canons themselves.

Choir

Choirs range from the sublime, like the Choir of King's College, Cambridge, to the corblimey of St Etheldreda's, Little Spawning. *The Oxford Dictionary of the Christian Church* defines a choir as a body

of singers assisting at Divine Service. Apparently they've been around since the 4th century.

The picture of the average choirboy – angelic, hair brushed, face scrubbed, well-behaved and a choral prodigy to boot – belongs more to fiction and fantasy than to reality. They chew gum, flick pellets, read football comics and play cards, while around them others try to worship God as best they can.

A problem with choirs, as with the organ, is that they can dominate the music to the point where the congregation doesn't have to bother . . . they can leave the choir and the organist to do it for them. On the other hand, there is nothing to compare with an anthem sung well, in the stillness of a beautiful church or cathedral.

Architecturally, the choir of a cathedral or abbey is a larger version of the chancel in parish churches.

Christopher, St

A giant, said to have carried an astonishingly heavy child over a river, his medal dangles in every taxi in Rome and on the chests of many who roam the world – he is, after all, the patron saint of travellers, and possibly of dangerous drivers.

In medieval times, to see Christopher's image was to be free from harm that day. He was often painted on the wall of the church immediately opposite the main door, so that believers could open the door, take a quick look, cross themselves, and go on their way, comprehensively insured.

Church Attendance

Some clergy are inclined to encourage attendance by sticking placards outside the building with messages such as 'Avoid the Christmas rush – come to church NOW' or 'CH..CH What is missing? U.R.'

Church Mouse

Poor as a church mouse. No-one is sure where the association of poor and church mouse first occurred.

In the book of Leviticus, the mouse is described to the people of Israel as being unclean among the creeping things that creep upon the earth, as are the weasel and the tortoise. Tortoises and weasels are not renowned churchgoers, however – unlike the church mouse who, for most of the year, depends on prayerbooks and songsheets for his diet. At harvest festival the church mouse has a grand time feasting on the sheaves of corn and other produce brought to church. John Betjeman describes the church mouse lamenting the numbers of people who come to church only at Harvest Festival time.

Robert Hawker, the famous mid-19th century vicar of Morwenstow, kept nine devout cats who regularly went to church with their master. One, forgetting itself, caught a mouse on Sunday, and, so the story goes, was promptly excommunicated for so foul a deed. Difficult to believe that this adorably dotty man, friend of all animals, would have been so severe – witness another story about him. When one of his old cassocks was used to dress a scarecrow, the result was disastrous – recognising the uniform of their protector, birds flocked in in anticipation of a hand-out and did great damage to the surrounding crop.

Churchyard

More battles have been fought over what may or may not be put in a churchyard than over some religious beliefs. Within the Church of England, parishioners and other people who die in the Parish have the right of burial in the churchyard, always provided there is still some space remaining. What they do not have the right to do is to cause unsuitable monuments to be erected in their memory. Strict regulations are delegated to the local priest, acting on behalf of the Chancellor of the Diocese. Undertakers, however, are very keen to satisfy the wildest dreams of their clients. Black marble headstones, angels, birdbaths, or headstones in the shape of a book or a heart, however desirable, are usually actively discouraged. Some connoisseurs of statuary are depressed at the lack of variety in monuments. They long for the days when choirs of angels were rendered in stone, when books and hearts witnessed to idiosyncratic tastes.

One of the most curious happenings ever reported in a cemetery concerned a man with a clipboard and stopwatch. This unlikely churchyard person lurked behind a gravestone, popping out every now and then to start or stop his watch. The local authority later confessed to carrying out a time and motion study of burials. Presumably they thought shaving a few seconds off Psalm 103, or dropping the coffin into the grave rather than reverently lowering it might save the ratepayers the odd pound or two on the rate.

Graveyards are not often places of pilgrimage. However, Highgate cemetery is regularly visited by pilgrims anxious to make sure that Karl Marx is indeed dead and buried there.

Clerestory

Pronounced 'clear story.' This is that part of the wall of a cathedral or church which is above the aisle roof and has a series of windows. 'Story' is thus really 'storey' – and the 'clere' what it says, these windows always being of clear glass, with the object of letting more light into the building.

His sermons were like the peace of God . . .
. . . they passed all understanding.

Anon

Cloud of Unknowing

A fog which the congregation may enter after a confusing sermon.

It's also a book on prayer and mysticism dating from the 14th century. No one knows the author, but that is not inappropriate as the author continually stresses the impossibility of knowing God by means of human reason.

The cloud of unknowing can, apparently, only be pierced by 'a sharp dart of love'. This is not a book for beginners.

Collect

A name for the special prayer for each Sunday and Holy Day in the year – from the word 'Collection' of prayers.

Collection – of Coins

There is an old story about a new vicar at a church keeping an eye on the proceedings so that he would know what to do.

During the hymn for the collection he noticed one old sidesman, as he marched up to the altar, take a coin out of the plate and slip it into his pocket. 'Funny', he thought to himself, but said nothing.

The next week he watched very closely and the same thing happened again. And on the third week – sure enough, yet again. This time, the vicar took the man aside and said, 'I couldn't help noticing, Mr Browning, that each week you take a coin off the plate and put it in your own pocket.'

'Ah, yes,' the man replied, 'But don't worry, Vicar, they all need a little encouragement and so I've been getting things off to a good start with this same half-a-crown for the past 15 years.'

Compline

A late evening service, said before retiring for the night. The word comes from the Latin *completus,* the past participle of *complere,* to complete.

In monastic days if Compline took too long to complete, even the most compliant monks were apt to complain.

Confirmation

The opportunity for an individual to make the promises of baptism his or her own. Always a solemn and meaningful ceremony, confirmation has not always been carried out in the traditional manner.

St Hugh, much-loved Bishop of Lincoln in the 12th century, covered such a huge diocese he often confirmed candidates from horseback. A brave and popular man, he defended his people against the royal foresters, refused to pay taxes to finance King Richard I's wars and showed great love and compassion towards lepers. It must have meant a lot to have been confirmed by him, even from the back of a horse.

Cotta

A white garment, worn by priests, it is shorter than a surplice and sometimes has frilly lace round the edges.

The story is told of a Roman Catholic monsignor who went to take a wedding in another town, and booked in at a very grand hotel. When he went up to his room at night, he discovered that the maid had laid out his pyjamas on one side of the double bed and his cotta on the other . . .

Crispin and Crispinian

The patron saints of cobblers and leather-workers since, nigh on 2,000 years ago, they plied their trade as shoemakers – rather than live off the faithful – while preaching the Word around ancient Italy.

Best remembered because of Henry V's public relations exercise on the eve of Agincourt: 'This day is called the Feast of Crispin . . .' – followed by no less than five additional mentions in the same speech.

Crosier

Sometimes spelt 'crozier'. This is a bishop's staff – not his chaplain, his chauffeur or secretary, but the staff he carries with him on ceremonial occasions. Opinions differ as to its origins. Some say it dates back to the soothsayers and augurs of Roman times who used such a rod or staff to trace the future. Others believe it's really just a fancy walking stick.

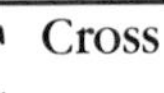

Cross

Christianity's great and unifying symbol.

The custom of 'touching wood' originally referred to The True Cross, the wooden cross on which Christ was crucified, whilst the superstition about walking under a ladder is said to go back to the ladder which was used to take down the body of Jesus after the Crucifixion.

Curate

An assistant priest working in a parish. The junior curate is usually straight from theological college, and a careful watch is kept on him. His sermons are often checked before he preaches them to the congregation. He is sometimes, quite inappropriately, given charge of the church youth club, and is often regarded with a mixture of admiration, anxiety and affection by older women in the parish. A second curacy is often seen as the step before taking charge of parish. A junior curate must steel himself for endless jokes about curate's eggs, which, like some curates, are good in parts.

Daily Service

First broadcast from St Martin in the Fields in 1924, the BBC's daily service could well be the longest-running radio programme in the world, apart from new bulletins. It is usually broadcast 'live' from All Souls, Langham Place, across the road from the BBC's headquarters, Broadcasting House.

Unusually for a live radio programme, members of the public are welcome to drift into the church and silently take part in the service. They should not, however, sing. This is the function of the BBC Singers.

David, St

St David of Wales is the only one of the four patron saints of the British Isles who was a native of the country which he represents. He lived in the 6th century and founded a monastery in the place that now bears his name. St David's Day is 1 March, when Welshmen are wont to sport daffodils or leeks in their button-holes.

The test of a preacher is that his congregation goes away saying not, 'What a lovely sermon!' but 'I will do something.'
St Francis de Sales

Deacon

From the Greek word meaning 'a servant', or 'to serve'. A deacon is the lowest of the three orders: bishop, priest then deacon.

Within the Church of England a man trained to be a priest is ordained deacon, and spends a year in that lowly role before being ordained priest. During that time he may not celebrate the Holy Communion, pronounce absolution from sins, or give the blessing.

Women can, of course, also be ordained as deacons although in the United Kingdom at least, this does not at present guarantee any further progress upward in the church ranks.

Dead Sea Scrolls

The collection of biblical manuscripts found in caves at Qumran near the Dead Sea between 1947 and 1956. The manuscripts date from around100 BC, and are about a thousand years older than the previous oldest Old Testament manuscript.

The scrolls include texts of many Old Testament books, psalms, commentaries and prayers, as well as material relating to the Jewish community to which they belonged. Their great value is as evidence of the accuracy of previously-known texts, as well as providing a picture of a Jewish community of the time of Christ.

The discovery was made by a young Arab, Muhammed el Dhib. He was idly throwing stones into the mouth of a cave when he heard the sound of breaking pottery. He fetched a friend and together they found pots with bundles of leather scrolls inside. It was the find of the century. But that's not an argument for stone throwing.

Dean

Usually a senior churchman in charge of a cathedral. But a Rural Dean is a senior clergyman with responsibility for administering a subdivision of an archdeaconry, the rural deanery.

The Dean or Provost of a cathedral is often a law unto himself, since cathedrals are independent of the diocesan structure – in the Anglican Church the bishop has to have the permission of the dean before entering the cathedral church of his diocese.

An Anglican Dean is appointed by the Crown, but within the Roman Catholic Church the Dean is subordinate to the bishop.

Rupert Brooke wrote these words:

Curates, long dust, will come and go
On lissom, clerical, printless toe;
And oft between the boughs is seen
The sly shade of a Rural Dean.

It's a great quote whatever it means. However, a Rural Dean makes sure that services are taken, temporary vacancies filled and generally fulfils the role of Uncle to the Deanery. He calls meetings of the clergy in his Deanery, works through the Deanery Synod and liaises with the diocesan authorities – an unenviable responsibility, given his other parish duties.

Defender of the Faith

Henry VIII asked Pope Leo X to grant him this title in return for having written a treatise on the seven sacraments in 1521. The Pope agreed and released a Papal Bull giving effect to the title.

Twenty-three years later, Parliament recognised 'Defender of the Faith' as a title to be applied to all succeeding monarchs. Which is why you can find the abbreviation 'Fid Def', an abbreviation of *Fidei Defensor*, on the coins of the realm.

Diet of Worms

This refers not to a feast for birds but is associated with Martin Luther. 'Diet' is a curious word – it means a legislative body. For example, a Diet was called semi-annually to order the affairs of the old Holy Roman Empire, an imperial Diet ruled the late 19th century German Empire, and today Japan still legislates through a Diet. The word originates from the medieval Latin word *dieta,* meaning 'a day', since originally it referred to a single daily session of a local court or legislature.

Worms is a city in Germany, twinned with St Albans, where Luther defended his doctrines before the Emperor Charles V and his advisers in 1521. This diet lasted for four months from 27 January to 25 May when Luther's teachings were formally condemned and everyone could feast again.

Divine Right

A topless lady once came into church. The congregation was aghast.

The vicar approached her. 'Madam,' he said, 'Your attire is inappropriate. I'm afraid I must ask you to leave.'

'But,' she replied, 'I have a divine right.'

'Madam,' he retorted, 'You have a divine left but that still does not give you the right to stay.'

DONNE, JOHN

Pronounced DUN as in 'Who dunnit'. Seventeenth-century Dean of St Paul's, preacher and poet. His *Hymn to God the Father* is full of puns on his own name Donne, as in 'When thou hast done, thou hast not done.'

What is especially interesting about John Donne is his transition from 'things of the flesh' to 'things of the spirit'. As a young man he loved elegant company – and, above all, elegant women. His early verse was therefore wordly – and positively erotic. As in *Going to Bed* . . .

Licence my roving hands, and let them go
Before, behind, between, above, below,
Oh my America! my new-found-land,
My kingdom, safeliest when with one man mann'd.

Later he turned to the metaphysical and the spiritual, and gave sermons which – though they were enormously influential – were also deadly dull!

EAGLE (Lectern)

A large brass bird which stands at the front of the nave – usually at the side, opposite the pulpit – bearing an enormous Bible on its back, and staring balefully at the congregation.

An eagle is the traditional symbolic bearer of the Good News, bringing the message of the Gospel to all the corners of the earth.

However, the mistake of a little Lancashire boy, more used to another kind of winged message-bearer, can be easily understood. For when he, for the first time in his life, spied a huge Eagle lectern in a cathedral, he turned to his father and cried, 'Eeh, Dad – just look at that bloomin' great pigeon!'

Easter

Easter is the chief festival of the Christian year when the Church remembers the Resurrection of Jesus, the Rising of the Son. This took place 'very early in the morning, while it was yet dark, on the first day of the week'. The Resurrection on Easter morning is thus the reason why Christians worship on a Sunday and not a Saturday, the Jewish Sabbath.

Easter eggs, with the chicken springing out of the shell, symbolise the Resurrection and new life. Easter bunnies and bonnets are also popular; so are Easter candles and chocolate eggs. Only the latter are eaten.

At one church service, eleven children were each asked to hold up a placard bearing the letters which together spell 'HAPPY EASTER'. Unfortunately, the girl holding the 'S' got cold feet.

The remaining ten were left proclaiming a slightly different message.

Ecumenical

A word to describe Christians from very different traditions getting together and working at common issues.

Some people fear that Christians sinking their differences will lose their individual character and become one great grey mass of religious clones. Others reckon that won't happen, because Christians are more likely to discover the riches in each other's traditions.

It's not long since the idea of the Archbishop of Canterbury and the Pope getting together and praying as equals would have been laughed out of court, but in 1966 that's exactly what happened. Now Christians work together in local radio Lent courses, industrial missions and much else, realising they're all in the same boat. And a small boat is the symbol of the ecumenical movement.

Elmo

Patron saint of seamen. Born Peter Gonzalez in 1190, Elmo became a Dominican, and sailed with Ferdinand III of Spain against the Moors. He then worked among Spanish sailors and was canonised on his death in 1246.

St Elmo's fire is the lightning-like electrical discharge seen at mastheads, and is widely believed to be a sign of the saint's protection.

Evensong

As its name suggests, Evensong, the main evening service of the Anglican Church, normally takes place in the evening – though some cathedrals decide to hold it in the afternoon. In winter, there are parish churches which follow suit – both to save on heating, and to enable the parishioners to see the beginning of the evening's television.

Evensong is sometimes not sung but said when, curiously, it is called Said Evensong, not Evensaid.

The service is based on the old monastic office or service of Vespers and Compline, and called 'Evening Prayer' in the Prayer Book.

Extempore Prayer

Prayers not from a book, but composed on the spur of the moment by the minister. A typical example might begin, 'O God, as you will have read in this morning's *Guardian* . . .'

Family

A line from a hymn goes, 'Peace, perfect peace/With dear ones far away.'

A nice description of family life?

Father of the Bride

In the old days, before the ASB (Alternative Service Book) was published, the bride's father was asked at weddings, 'Who giveth this woman to be married to this man?'

A most unfair question, since no provision was made in the prayer book for any answer.

The bride's father shuffled forward, and somehow got hold of his daughter's right hand – no mean feat since she was facing to the front. He then handed said right hand to the priest, who passed it to the bridegroom. All very symbolic – the bride's father handing responsibility for the bride to the bridegroom, via the priest.

Amid the tensions of the wedding service, it often proves difficult for the bride's father to remain silent when the question is put.

One Sergeant Major, trained from his youth to answer any question with an excess of diligence, attended the wedding rehearsal on the event of the great day. Patiently coached by the vicar to say nothing when asked, 'Who giveth this woman to be married to this man?' he agreed to say nothing, and simply do the business with his daughter's right hand.

At the wedding, all was going smoothly. The bride had removed her gloves on arrival at the chancel step. She had remembered to lose her bouquet to the chief bridesmaid.

Then came the question, 'Who giveth this woman . . . ?

Her father, forgetting the lesson of the previous evening, and reverting to the habits of a lifetime, snapped to attention with a tremendous clatter.

'I do, sah!' he shouted.

His daughter was heard to remark in something louder than the average stage whisper, 'Oh shut up, Dad.'

Feast of Fools

A medieval holiday celebrated near the start of the year, in which laity and junior clergy took a full part, ridiculing their elders, but not necessarily betters. They sent up the pomp and solemnity of meetings and services. Bawdy songs were sung and faces painted.

A leader – called Boy Bishop, Mock King or Lord of Misrule – was elected to preside over the merriment and no-one was safe from ridicule.

Not everyone saw the funny side and the practice was banned by the Council of Basel in 1431. Even so, traces of the idea can still be found in Christmas revels at theological colleges, when staff and dignitaries fall victim to the sharp wits of the students.

The camel never sees its own hump, but its neighbour's hump is ever before its eyes

Arab proverb

Feast of Stephen

It was this feast on which Good King Wenceslas looked out when the snow lay round about, deep and crisp and even.

However, it does not mean that Stephen was holding an open-air banquet or picnic in the middle of winter. Rather, it is telling us that the King was staring out of his window on St Stephen's Day. And St Stephen's Day is the day after Christmas, 26 December – Boxing Day – which is why we sing this carol at Christmas.

Stephen was the first Christian martyr, and we are told that he had the face of an angel.

FETE

It would be easy to think that the annual fete or garden party ran Christmas and Easter a close third in importance in the Church's year. They can become an obsession . . . The last trestle table has barely been packed away before plans are being made for a bigger and better fete next year.

Fetes raise money, strengthen the glue that binds Christians together and provide opportunities for the rest of the community to see that Christians are not all two-headed ogres. They also provide opportunities for faith, selfless devotion and sacrifice beyond the ancient martyrs' worst nightmares.

Picking the date is the most hazardous of decisions facing the fete committee. Long debates rage: is it in order to pray for clement weather, ('Shall we just have a word of prayer about that, Vicar?'). Is it right both to pray for fine weather *and* to take out insurance? Shall we get a DJ from the local radio station to open the fete? Won't he charge a fee? What *is* a DJ anyway? Where are the skittle balls? What about posters? Can we get the police to put out cones outside the vicarage to prevent double parking? Can I run the cake stall this year, Vicar? The checklist is endless.

But when the great day dawns and the arguments are stilled, the cakes multiply in yet another modern miracle, the Scouts honour their promise to clear up the litter, and it all seems worthwhile. When the Young Wives make it up with the Men's Society, the Brownies dance their Gypsy Dance and the child that was lost is found; when the pantomime horse forgets its internal quarrel and gets on with making people laugh, you see the point of it all.

At its peculiarly-English best, there's nothing like a church fete.

FLEA

An insect which appears, quite by chance and totally unexpectedly, when certain people are reading aloud the second chapter of St Matthew.

That's the bit where the angel of the Lord appears to Joseph in a dream, saying, 'Arise and take the young child and his mother and flee into Egypt.'

FLOWER ROTA

A gift to comedy writers. Who's on the list? Who's responsible for the flowers by the altar? Flower rota battles can be bloodier than the War of The Spanish Succession.

Brass-cleaning runs the flower rota a close second.

The tradition of beautifying a church for worship is a very long one, stretching back past stained glass and embroidery to wall-paintings. Many churches mount flower festivals when the skills of the flower arrangers are displayed to great advantage – often accompanied by cream teas, concerts and handicrafts fairs. In short, they tend to turn into full-scale celebrations of God-given gifts.

On the other hand, where dissent reigns because Mrs Molestrangler's particular pitch by the font has been usurped by Mrs Gutbucket who has only just arrived in the parish, diplomacy and tact are required to avert total war. It's not enough for a feeble vicar to assert that Mrs Gutbucket's economy of style with two bullrushes and a drooping geranium is a searing testament to the predicament facing our planet – ecologically speaking, you understand.

FONT

Not a bird-bath, but a large – often carved stone – water container, like an elevated pond, in which baptisms are carried out.

'Font' comes from the Latin word meaning 'spring' or 'fountain'.

In the early Church, converts to Christianity were baptised by total immersion in running water, preferably in a river. Fine, if you lived in one of the countries bordering the Mediterranean in the second century, before pollution gained a hold. But hands up who wants to be totally immersed in the Rhine or the Thames below Cross Ness Sewage Treatment Works.

Originally, the font was sunk below the church floor and the new Christian was either immersed or had water poured over him. As infant baptism became more prevalent, the font was raised and became the piece of church furniture we know today. However, in many Baptist churches, baptism is still by total immersion, so the pool is let into the floor of the church.

In many churches the font is located near the door of the church, symbolising the entry of the newly-baptised into membership of the Church.

Many fonts have covers over them to prevent birds which may have dropped in to the church through a window or a hole in the roof from dropping in . . . !

The covers are also useful sites for flower arrangements.

FOX, GEORGE

The founder of the Society of Friends, or Quakers, or Great British Chocolate Makers (– famous Quakers have included Joseph Rowntree and George Cadbury, as well as the prison reformer Elizabeth Fry).

The Friends came into being in the 17th century and very soon many of them moved to the United States where one of their number, William Penn, founded Pennsylvania.

Fox also took frequent missionary journeys to Ireland, the West Indies, North America and Holland. However, he lived in England, and was born – very dangerously for one of his name – in the great hunting county of Leicestershire.

The central doctrine of the Friends is the 'inner light', and they have no set forms of worship, no ministry and no sacraments. Their meetings are silent until some member feels moved to speak, or pray, or sing. They refuse military service as fighting participants, being pledged to pacificism, but as stretcher-bearers and the like have repeatedly served heroically in the thick of the action.

When the fox preaches, look to your geese.
German proverb

Friars

Most friars do not behave in the least like Friar Tuck. They are members of mendicant orders and don't hold property in common – unlike the monks, who do. So friars beg or work for their living.

The different orders were established in the Middle Ages. Like cassocks, friars are colour-coded to help you tell them apart. There are Grey Friars (Franciscans), Black Friars (Dominicans) and White Friars (Carmelites). All very confusing – like snooker before you've learnt the rules.

Funeral

The last goodbye to someone you loved, hated or didn't really know very well, funerals are an enormous challenge to the conscientious priest. It's vital that they should be well-prepared, decently organised and sensitively taken. There's nothing worse than getting the deceased's name wrong, having the grave dug too small to accept the coffin, or forgetting to be there at the right time.

Every vicar has a fund of amusing stories about funerals. One involves a young priest who was riding along on top of a bus when he noticed a crowd outside a church, complete with hearse, limousine, and anxious looks by the score.

Doing the decent thing, he hopped off the bus, established that here was a funeral without the promised priest, leapt into some borrowed robes and took the service himself. He finished his career as Dean of a cathedral, and retired with a knighthood.

In America, it's wise to start saving for your funeral before you're born. Indeed, so high are the prices there that many people simply cannot afford to die, which might be why they go on living so long. It may also be the reason for the development of cryogenic life suspension techniques, in which the client is deep-frozen in liquid nitrogen and kept in suspended animation until either the funeral fees reduce or mighty science finds a cure for his final ailment.

Funeral Director

Sometimes known as the undertaker. In the United States, such people are known as morticians. They can be both masters of merriment and magicians of the macabre.

Some of the funniest people are funeral directors.

One south London undertaker was very good at his job – never ripped off his clients and was terrific with bereaved families. Out of sight of his clients, however, he was a first-class entertainer.

Once obliged to spend a short time in hospital, he found himself in a ward full of heart and chest cases. As soon as he was up and about, he lost no time in measuring them all up, making copious notes on each and every one – and he left them all with promotional literature for the undertaking business which he happened to represent.

This may sound macabre, but the effect of this on all who could see the funny side was electric. The others presumably died. Either way, he couldn't lose.

Traditionally, many undertakers started work in the carpenter's shop of a building company, which is why there is such a connection between builders and stone-masons, carpenters and undertakers – some undertakers even like to be known as funeral furnishers.

The range of the undertaker's services is almost beyond belief but sometimes the best-laid plans of mice and morticians go awry.

At a crematorium chapel, where all the hymn accompaniment and incidental music was on tape, someone hadn't done his homework. When the minister asked the mourners to stand and sing the 23rd Psalm to the setting *Crimond*, the music that emerged from the PA system wasn't Crimond at all, but *The Tennessee Waltz*.

Under this stone, Reader, survey
Dead Sir John Vanbrugh's house of clay.
Lie heavy on him, Earth! for he
Laid many heavy loads on thee!

Epitaph on Sir John Vanbrugh,
architect of Blenheim Palace

Gabriel

The angel or archangel who came to announce to Mary that she was to have a baby. He is thus the patron saint of weight-watchers – because he came down to announce.

Gaiters

These were worn at one time by archdeacons, presumably to protect their venerable limbs from venomous serpents while they inspected churchyards. They can't have been too comfortable, for there's a limerick that goes:

There was an Archdeacon who said,
'May I take off my gaiters in bed?'
The Bishop said, 'No,
You must wear them, you know,
Until the day you are dead.'

GALILEE

A Scotsman went on a trip to the Holy Land with some friends, and went to see the Sea of Galilee, where Jesus walked upon the water. He walked down to the shore, where a boat was moored. A board next to the boat said 'Trips across the lake: £30.'

'Hoots mon!' said the Scotsman. 'If that's how much it costs, it's nae wonder he walked!'

GARDEN OF EDEN

In the Garden of Eden, it wasn't the apple on the tree that was the problem, but the pair on the ground.

GEORGE, ST

Just how did the dragon-slaying, maiden-saving soldier from somewhere in the Middle East become the patron saint of England?

For St George, whose red cross emblem is the centre of our national flag, was not an Englishman at all. He was some wretched foreign chap, who never once set foot in this country but lived in some far-off part of Asia Minor, where 1,600 years ago he rescued a damsel in distress and removed her from the clutches of a fierce and fiery dragon before valiantly killing the beast.

The English connection took time to develop. George became a cult saint for Britons fighting in the Crusades and Richard I (1189–99)

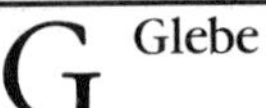

placed himself and his army under the saint's protection. Nearly a century and a half later (and about 1,000 years after George's death) Edward III officially proclaimed him England's patron saint. But it took Henry V to clinch the matter for all true and right-thinking Englishmen!

GLEBE

Land that the incumbent or priest of a parish can cultivate himself. If the priest doesn't farm the glebe, it can be let out to others, and the income applied to the maintenance of the clergy. One vicarage had 65 acres of glebe and cultivating it would have been a full-time job – 'Sorry, he can't come to the phone, he's ploughing, cultivating, drilling the glebe.'

A priest lived in a splendid vicarage which stood in just one acre of ground. The grass alone took four to five hours to mow every eight days in summer, and the wilderness threatened on every side. He couldn't afford to pay gardeners, maids, cook and butler, though the vicarage had been designed with them in mind. It was a lovely house, a great garden, but quite beyond his powers to farm or maintain. Times without number he pressed the bell for the servant, but no-one came.

'When in the sultry glebe I faint,' runs a verse from a hymn. The writer was probably fainting from too much scything of grass in the glebe. It's a lovely word, glebe, but it will probably come to mean less and less.

GOD

A famous prayer speaks of 'the peace of God which passeth all understanding'. But many people would think that it is not just a piece but the whole of Him which is beyond our comprehension. Indeed He is very helpfully defined as 'The Father incomprehensible, the Son incomprehensible, and the Holy Ghost incomprehensible' in the Athanasian Creed (one of the three ancient creeds of the Christian church, attributed to – but certainly written long after – Athanasius, fourth-century bishop of Alexandria).

To be like Christ is to be a Christian.
William Penn

GODPARENT

These are witnesses or sponsors who undertake to bring up a newly-baptised child in the Christian faith. That's the hope, and the theory. The practice is often very different.

Godparents are often chosen for their wealth in the hope that they will shower the child with expensive presents every birthday and

Christmas. Often they live hundreds of miles away from their godchild – sometimes on the other side of the world. How anyone living that far away can help to bring up the child in the faith is something of a mystery.

In the end, it's usually the parents, rather than the godparents who influence the child, for good or ill.

Good Friday

One of the most holy days in the Christian calendar. Three-hour services and hot cross buns for those who stayed the course characterised past observance of the day.

Nowadays Good Friday is marked by the singing of Stainer's *Cruxifixion,* processions of witness, street theatre or passion plays, and the opening of shops, stores and out-of-town shopping centres.

A company of Christians was into the first scene of a street theatre passion play when the director noticed something was terribly wrong. 'We've forgotten the cross,' was the anxious cry, and four men were despatched to fetch the wooden cross from the church two streets away.

Gospel

Good news, from the old English word *godspel*.

When the musical *Godspell* first opened in London, nuns demonstrated outside the theatre in protest at such a blasphemous representation of the good news.

Grave Humour

'In the name of the Father, and of the Son, and into the hole he goes.' This example of funeral fun probably dates from the 19th century when it was not unknown for priests to be so drunk that they fell into graves at funerals.

The Reverend James Adams, who won the Victoria Cross for gallantry during the Afghan War, was burying some cholera victims when he stepped backwards and fell into an open grave. There is no suggestion that *he* was drunk at the time, and nobody laughed.

In foul weather, the boards at the side of an open grave can become extremely slippery, so if your vicar plummets into the grave, it may be due to ease of access rather than an excess of alcohol.

Gutenberg, Johann

Johann Gutenberg invented a system of movable type which enabled whole pages to be printed at a time. His father's surname was Gensfleich – in English, 'Gooseflesh' – and, not wanting to be remembered as the printer of the Gooseflesh Bible, Johann changed his name to his mother's maiden name, Gutenberg.

Born in Mainz in 1396, Gutenberg was a goldsmith by trade. He proved to be more of an inventor than a financial wizard. Despite the success of his printing process, he became bankrupt in 1455, just a year after printing the Roman Catholic Bible or Vulgate.

Gutenberg's invention was probably more significant than that of electronic typesetting today. His process could produce in one day what it had previously taken a year to print.

Harold

According to some small children, one of the names of God. As in the Lord's Prayer – 'Our Father, who art in heaven, Harold be thy name.'

Harvest Festival

Less well-known as the Feast of St Pumpkin, one of the most popular in the Church's calendar. The custom of a harvest festival goes back to Jewish tradition, when the people were required to bring the first fruits of their labours to the priest as a thanks offering to God.

It is an occasion to fill the church with wheat sheaves, fruit, flowers, vegetables, tinned hula hoops in tomato sauce and baked beans to celebrate another harvest safely gathered in.

At one service, crowded with hordes of children and parents, the children were asked to suggest the names of various foods beginning with all the different letters of the alphabet. They were quick off the mark with A for apple, B for bread, C for carrot, but when at length they came to Q, the silence was deafening. Eventually, however, one little girl shot up her hand, and, to the delight of the congregation but the acute embarrassment of her mother, proudly proclaimed 'Q for cucumber'.

Hassocks

Sometimes called kneelers, these are designed to ease the pain felt when kneeling in church.

Where hassocks are made with care and love, they are an ornament to the local church – as well as a way of keeping holy knees in good condition.

Hassocks is also a village in Sussex, north of Brighton.

Believing in God means getting down on your knees.
Martin Luther

Hats

St Paul advised the Christians at Corinth that women should cover the heads during worship. Respectable women veiled their hair in first-century Corinth, and Paul was anxious that the new believers should not acquire a doubtful reputation. The tradition remains, more within the Roman Catholic Church and certain extreme evangelical churches.

One church-goer was pursued by one of the leaders of her church because she refused to wear a hat to services. She wasn't into hats, and became so incensed at what she felt was persecution that she turned up at church in a bikini just to make the point that it was no part of the church's business to specify what was and was not acceptable wear.

There is a problem with hats at communion services. If a brim is too broad, it is extremely difficult to tell whether or not the chalice or communion cup has connected with the lips, and if it has, whether one is about to drown the communicant in wine. A small point, but one not always considered when ladies choose the hat to wear to mass or communion.

Herbert, George

A 17th-century Anglican priest, pastor and poet who wrote one of the very best Christian poems in the English language beginning 'Love bade me welcome.'

Born in 1593 towards the end of the reign of Queen Elizabeth I, he died in 1633, at Bemerton in Wiltshire where he was the parish priest.

Four of his poems are now well-known hymns: *Let all the world in every corner sing; King of Glory, King of Peace; The God of Love my Shepherd is* and *Teach me my God and King.* The last-named includes the verse:

A servant with this clause
Makes drudgery divine,
Who sweeps a room as for thy laws
Makes that and the action fine.

However, Herbert himself was not, one suspects, a great sweeper of rooms, living as he did at Bemerton very simply with six domestic servants and two assistant curates.

High Church

The Catholic end of the Church of England spectrum.

This is a church which delights in elaborate ceremonies and ritual, where there is much colour and movement, beautifully choreographed; much swinging of incense; gorgeous and glorious apparel on the priest and on the altar; the ringing of bells in the sanctuary; the lighting and carrying of candles; much genuflecting and bowing; much chanting and singing, maybe to the music of Mozart and Schubert; many statues and effigies; servers galore, both young and not-so-young; ancient missals; and maybe even the wearing and doffing of birettas. High churches love processions with candles and banners, and carrying statues about. They go to town on Festivals and Saints' Days and all kinds of Holy Days.

High Church people owe much of their vigour to members of the Oxford Movement who, from 1833, began their struggle to reassert the Catholic tradition. They emphasised the importance of ritual and the value of ministry, especially amongst the needy of Victorian slums. Many of their missions and settlements remain to serve today's poor. It is largely due to the Oxford Movement, led by John Newman, that our churches look as they do today – for they helped sweep away 18th-century furnishings and brought about a return to what they saw as truly Gothic interiors.

We do the works, but God works in us the doing of the works.

St Augustine of Hippo

Hippo, St Augustine of

Augustine's mother was St Monica who tried to bring him up as a Christian, but he found her very trying. At sixteen he went to Carthage to complete his education, and spent the next fourteen years living with a young woman of unknown name who bore him a son. He was devoted to them and always loved them.

Always very aware of his very human urges, Augustine once prayed, famously: 'Oh Lord, make me chaste – but not yet', thus endearing himself to millions who came after him. Later his mother's devotion to him was well rewarded when he and his son were baptised together on Easter Eve in AD 387. Promotion came fast – he was consecrated Bishop of Hippo, in North Africa, in AD 396.

Augustine of Hippo became one of the greatest bishops in the history of the church, and wrote books galore. Over 100 of these survive, with more than 200 letters and over 500 sermons, among them being some of the greatest of all Christian documents.

Holy Fools

St Paul's words in his first letter to the Christians at Corinth are worth careful consideration: 'If any man among you seems to be wise in this world, let him become a fool, that he may be wise. For the wisdom of this world is foolishness with God.' Later he writes, 'We are fools for Christ's sake, but you are wise in Christ; we are weak but you are strong; you are honourable but we are despised.'

The tradition of holy foolishness is extremely long and dates back to the prophets of Israel who were thought foolish because of the lengths to which they would go, and the risks they would take, in speaking the word God had given them. St Francis of Assisi has been called God's Fool because of the clarity with which he saw what God wanted him to do.

In the United States Holy Fools – thousands of clergy and laity – are exploring disciplines such as clowning, mime, puppet, dance and storytelling as important elements of church life.

Holy Fools in this country are rediscovering the value of humour and foolishness within the church structures, to the amazement of many inside the church walls and the delight of many who thought that to believe in God was terribly terribly dull and boring!

Hope

'Hope is a good breakfast,' said Sir Francis Bacon. And with a name like that, he should have known . . .

Adam and Eve had many advantages, but the principal one was that they escaped teething.

Mark Twain

Hymns

These are the traditional songs of the church, and have been composed in every century. They remain very popular, and among the best known are the Wembley favourite ***Abide with Me*** and the Promenaders' delight ***Jerusalem***. They have mainly survived, unscathed, the passage of time and changing use of language, unlike two of the earliest known hymns entitled ***Bridle of Colts Untamed*** and ***Up Maidens*** . . .

Favourite characters in hymns include a teddy ('Gladly my cross I'd bear'), another furry animal ('That child she bear'), a brave insect ('Valiant Be'), members of the Civil Service ('Ye servants of the Lord each in his office wait'), an extraordinary woman ('Amazing Grace'), and a helpful member of the criminal classes ('Thy friendly crook shall give me aid').

Christmas hymns are traditionally sung to different words in each generation. For example, 'While shepherds washed their socks by night' in the 1940s became in the 1960s:

While shepherds watched the box by night,
All tuned to BBC,
The Angel of the Lord came down,
And switched to ITV.

A 1930s example would be:

Hark! The herald angels sing
Mrs Simpson's pinched our king,
Peace on earth and mercy mild,
Wasn't Mr Baldwin wild?

ICHABOD

The Philistines had been troublesome again. They had attacked the Israelites and slaughtered 30,000 footmen – or so it says in the Authorised Version of the Bible, footmen being infantry rather than lowly servants paid to say, 'You rang, sir.'

To add insult to injury they captured the ark of God, and when old Eli heard the bad news, he fell off his seat and died. His pregnant daughter-in-law heard the news that her husband had been killed and that Eli had died just as her child was born so she called her new-born son Ichabod, a word meaning 'The glory has departed from Israel.'

INCENSE

Holy smoke, produced by burning aromatic resins on charcoal in a thurible or censer, a metal container of extraordinary complexity.

The Old Testament records many rules and regulations regarding the offering of incense, a smell pleasing to God – perhaps a refreshing change from the smell of burnt offerings of meat.

Incense and its use are symbolic for those who have eyes to see beyond the symbolism. Smoke ascending is a picture of prayer rising to the throne of God. It's a sign of God being about the place; as the carol puts it: 'incense owns a Deity nigh'.

The Warden of a Theological College, a godly and sensitive man, insisted that incense was burnt in the chapel at least twice a year. Since students might leave the college and go on to 'High' Church parishes, it was vital that they discovered beforehand whether they were allergic to incense.

Unfortunately with such infrequent use, no-one was sufficiently skilled to regulate the practice. So the anxious or cautious beginner would conjure a pathetic wisp of smoke from the censer, whilst the enthusiast or the ill-advised would cause the whole sanctuary and those within it to disappear in a pall of choking aromatic mist.

INCUMBENT

Not to be confused with recumbent, the incumbent is that priest who is in charge of a parish.

He may be a rector, vicar or a curate or priest in charge. Indeed there are now some parishes where he is a she, and a woman deacon is, for all practical purposes, in charge.

I like the silent church before the service begins better than any preaching.

Ralph Waldo Emerson

INDUCTION

The 'putting-in' of that person who is to be in charge of a parish.

The induction is into the temporalities, or practicalities, of his work. It follows the institution of a priest into the pastoral and spiritual responsibilities, usually carried out by the bishop.

The archdeacon takes the future incumbent, leads him to the altar where he will celebrate the Eucharist, lays his hand on the key of the church door, causes him to toll the bell, to stand by the font, and leads him to his stall where he will lead the people in prayer.

One priest – on being given the key of the church with which he was required to lock the door on the outside, then unlock it and let himself back into the building – admitted nearly giving in to the delicious temptation to lock everyone inside the church, throw away the key and run for it.

Alas, he didn't.

INQUISITION

A nasty way of suppressing nasty habits, beliefs and practices within the Church.

In the first centuries of the Christian faith, death could be exacted as a punishment for heresy. Excommunication – the cutting-off of the condemned from all the activities and blessings of church membership – was a less extreme punishment, and is still available to the churches. The hunting-down of heretics within the Holy Roman Empire was entrusted to officials of the state by Frederick II in 1232, but Pope Gregory IX claimed this was the church's business and set papal inquisitors to the task.

Heresy was believed by some to be such a vile condition that any 'cure', including torture, was thought preferable. So we have the unedifying spectacle of the rack, the fire and the thumbscrew being used to convince people of the error of their ways and beliefs. Not a striking example of the love of God at work, you may think.

The Spanish Inquisition was probably the fiercest example, aimed as it was at converts from Islam and Judaism, and then at Protestants. One source estimates that 2,000 people were burnt at the stake under the Grand Inquisitor, Torquemada.

Men must be governed by God or they will be ruled by tyrants.

William Penn

JACOB

The name Jacob means 'A heel', and the Old Testament Jacob was certainly that. He was the twister who deprived his brother Esau of his birthright.

The Bible says that 'Jacob sod pottage', which sounds revolting. It also says that Esau was a hairy man while Jacob was a smooth man. He therefore put goatskins on his hands and the smooth of his neck so that his blind father might feel and bless him instead of his brother. Having been such a snake it's very appropriate that he is also famous for his ladder – which he saw in a dream leading up to Heaven, with angels pottering up and down. Then God spoke and said that Jacob's descendants would be spread over all the earth, before they were gathered together again into the Promised Land . . . and God changed his name to Israel!

Incidentally, while Jacob slept and dreamed, a stone served as his pillow. Tradition has it that this is the Stone of Scone, on which Scottish kings were crowned and which now rests snugly under the Coronation Chair in London's Westminster Abbey.

Jehovah's Witnesses

Members of a sect founded by an American draper from Pittsburg, Charles Russell, who studied the scriptures and concluded that the end of the world would come in 1914.

It didn't, of course, but the Great War started instead.

In 1884, Russell founded the Watch Tower Bible and Tract Society. *The Watch Tower* is still published, and Jehovah's Witnesses often canvass door to door, handing out copies of their publication and beginning doorstep debates, 'Aren't you worried about the state of the world?'

A good beginning but, alas, no good end – unless, of course, you happen to be a Jehovah's Witness. For when the end of the world *does* finally arrive, only the elect of Jehovah – his Witnesses – will be saved.

Jesus

Jesus is the hero of the Bible, especially the New Testament, and even more especially the four Gospels of Matthew, Mark, Luke and John. He is the Church's One Foundation and the subject of numerous great works of art, including Holman Hunt's *The Light of the World.* In music He is the Joy of Man's Desiring.

Jesus is also leading character in the great musical shows *Godspell* and *Jesus Christ Superstar,* and in the 1977 four-part television film *Jesus of Nazareth,* Dennis Potter's *Son of Man* and the Hollywood blockbusters *King of Kings* (1927) and *The Greatest Story Ever Told* (1965). In the last-named Jesus was played by a Scandinavian, John the Baptist by Charlton Heston, Pilate by Telly Savalas, and the Centurion at the foot of the cross by John Wayne. Near the end of the film, when it came to the Centurion's big line, the director pleaded, 'No, no, John. Say it with awe.'

'O.K. man,' said Wayne. 'Aw, truly this was the Son of God.'

Truth is God's daughter.
Spanish proverb

Jews

God's chosen people.

A rabbi once said, 'When you think what the Jews have suffered, they should be called God's foolish people.' And maybe the degree to which they have suffered has given birth to their spectacular sense of humour.

Rabbi Lionel Blue tells this story: 'If a Jewish person met a Nazi in the street, he had to get off the pavement into the gutter. There's this Jew walking along a street in Berlin, and a Nazi officer approaches. The Jew stays on the pavement and the Nazi looks at him and shouts, "Schwein!"

The Jew raises his hat and says "Cohen!" '.

Jonah

This Old Testament character refused to go to the city of Nineveh. Instead, he caught a ship sailing in the opposite direction and had a whale of a time.

Joseph

Star of musical by Andrew Lloyd Webber, *Joseph and his Amazing Technicolour Dreamcoat.* Also youngest and most tedious of the sons of Jacob, who so upset his brothers that they took his multi-coloured coat and dumped him in a deep pit. Then the story gets really confusing.

A party of Midianite merchants with an eye to the main chance rescued Joseph and sold him to a bunch of Ishmaelites for twenty pieces of silver, the going rate for seventeen-year-olds found in pits. The Ishmaelites were on their way to sell camel-loads of perfume and aftershave to the Egyptians.

His brothers, in the meantime, dipped Joseph's coat of many colours in goat's blood so that his father would think he'd been eaten by wolves or hyenas, or worse. Jacob was very upset, tore his clothes, put on an old sack and wouldn't speak to anyone.

Meanwhile, the Midianites (or was it the Ishmaelites?) had arrived in Egypt and among their bargain offers for the Egyptians was Joseph. Potiphar, captain of the King of Egypt's guard, bought Joseph who, after a spell in prison on a trumped-up charge of attempted rape, eventually became chief minister to Pharaoh, was reunited with his brothers, saved Egypt from famine and lived to a ripe old age.

Julian of Norwich

This Julian was a woman, a recluse usually known as Mother or the Lady Julian of Norwich, who lived in the 14th century and is now commemorated in Norwich Cathedral. She saw visions and wrote *Revelations of Divine Love,* a wonderful book of Christian piety. One of her visions was of a little thing the size of a hazel nut, on the palm of her hand, round like a ball, which inspired her to think gloriously of the love of God, for in the example of this tiny kernel, Mother Julian discerned the whole world of God's creation.

Julian was born in 1343 – about the same time as Chaucer – and, it is thought, was educated by the nuns of Carrow Priory, on the outskirts of Norwich. On 8 May, 1373, during severe illness, she received a series of 'showings' from God. From this grew her life of religious devotion, walled up in a cell at St Julian's Church in Norwich (from which, it seems, she took her name). There, over a period of 20 years, she wrote her remarkable and inspiring book, the first in English to be written by a woman.

St Julian's transcending faith in God and His love shines through this still marvellously accessible work, and one sentence in particular has become familiar as a beacon of hope: 'Sin is behovely, but all shall be well and all shall be well and all manner of thing shall be well'.

Jumble Sale

To see all human life – indeed, to witness miracles – go to a church jumble sale.

Here are mounds of clothes, heaps of books, pairs of braces, cracked teapots, old Alma Cogan records, chipped plates, saucerless cups, indescribable long thin objects with lumps on the end . . . mystery made flesh. See the stalwarts who sell fur coats back to the Eskimos who gave them, who can tell from looking at a string vest what size it is, who claim without blinking an eye that Harold Robbins' earliest potboiler is just the read for Aunt Maud.

Here's the customer thirsting for a scorched art-deco lampshade and a pair of very second-hand long johns. There's a helper who fears a colleague has just sold her crocodile-skin handbag and all her credit cards to the man from Social Security. Here are tea-sellers, washers-up and a man asking for the joker from last year's bargain pack of cards.

And here's the miracle . . . a profit of hundreds of pounds to heat the church for one more week, buy a missionary a bicycle for the African bush, feed starving children and buy a wheelchair for a housebound mum.

Keswick Convention

This is an annual opportunity for Evangelicals to meet together in Keswick to pray, study, listen to addresses – and swap them.

Founded in 1875, its aim is to promote practical holiness. It is one of many such events, of which Royal Week in Cornwall and Downs Bible Week in Sussex are examples.

Sunday clears away the rust of the whole week.
Joseph Addison

Kiss of Peace

One of the present Archbishop of Canterbury's sermon stories is about a teenager noticing in the window of a book-shop a volume called *How to Hug.* He rushed in to buy, only to discover when he had paid his money and got outside, that it was one of the volumes of an encyclopaedia.

Knox, John

Sixteenth-century Scottish reformer.

In 1547 Knox became preacher in St Andrew's, and was captured by the French during one of their regular wars with Scotland. On his release he returned to England and became chaplain to Edward VI. When 'Bloody Mary' came to the throne he left for the Continent, unable to contemplate the prospect of a woman as sovereign.

A quarrelsome man, Knox worked for a short while among English refugees in Frankfurt before being forced to leave after an argument over Sunday worship.

He spent some time in his native Scotland but persecution forced him to flee again, and he worked at the English church in Geneva where he published the tract that has so endeared him to feminists and supporters of the ordination of women, *The First Blast of the Trumpet against the Monstrous Regiment of Women.* In this he argued that for a woman to rule was against God's will and contrary to nature. Elizabeth I was not amused and refused to let him pass through England on his way home in 1559.

Lady Chapel

Not a member of the aristocracy, nor a chapel reserved for members of a particular sex. But, in a church or cathedral, a chapel dedicated to our Lady, the Blessed Virgin Mary.

Lamentations

A none-too-cheerful Old Testament book commemorating the destruction of the Temple in 586 BC. Not recommended to readers of a depressed state of mind.

Lay Reader

A man or woman, not dog-collared, licensed by a bishop to take services. The office dates from 1866 and can involve a great deal of varied – and unpaid – work.

Like bishops, cardinals and popes, lay readers are colour-coded – they wear a blue scarf.

Lent

The 40 days before Easter, starting on Ash Wednesday. A period of fasting and abstinence. In former times meat, fish and eggs were strictly forbidden. Thus, on Shrove Tuesday (the last day before Lent), all remaining eggs were used in making pancakes. Eggs would not then reappear until Easter when they would be laid on the dining-room table for breakfast.

Nowadays, the Lenten fast is not so strictly observed. Someone might give up smoking, for example, but possibly with the intention of saving the money in order to buy a lighter when the 40 days are over.

Levi, Sons of

Levi was one of the sons of Jacob in the Book of Genesis. He seems to have had extraordinarily effective genes, because his denim-clad descendents can still be found all over the earth.

Litany

A neglected set of prayers, devised by Thomas Cranmer when England was at war with Scotland in 1544. Henry VIII ordered the use of the Litany in processions. It was to be used on Sundays, Wednesdays and Fridays after morning prayer or Matins.

The fact that England is no longer at war with Scotland cannot be entirely attributed to the saying or singing of the Litany.

Low Church

The other end of the churchmanship spectrum from High Church. Low Church is a term applied today to Evangelicals, for whom anything that smacks of Rome and ritual is difficult to countenance.

A belief in the inspiration of scripture and a low emphasis on the sacramental, characterise today's low churchperson. Personal conversion and salvation by faith are the touchstones of this strand of belief and practice.

John Newton and Charles Simeon were early Evangelicals or Low Churchmen and combined personal piety with a zeal for social reform.

Luke, St

Matthew, Mark and John are very popular names for boys today. But not so popular is Luke, which sounds rather like the name of a character in a Western.

Luke in the Bible was a doctor – the 'beloved physician' – and so his Gospel describes twice as many healings as the others. He is patron saint, naturally, of doctors and surgeons, and also of artists.

Manse

The house in which a minister of religion lives.

Whereas Church of England clergy live in rectories, vicarages or clergy houses – unless they're really posh, in which case they live in deaneries or palaces – ministers of Nonconformist churches, and Scottish Presbyterian in particular, live in manses. Roman Catholic clergy often live in presbyteries. It's all very confusing. The manse is usually owned by the church, and the minister lives rent-and rates-free, because it's an official house where he or she is required to live.

In some traditions in the past, the manse was furnished by the Church, a practice that often meant it being filled with all kinds of junk furniture that nobody else would be seen dead with. Nowadays, ministers have their own furniture and take it with them when they go.

The practice of generous people leaving all kinds of worn-out junk to the clergy or the church has not entirely died out. A minister was given a two-stroke lawnmower which, he was assured, had many years' use left in it. It was such a pig to start that he took his exercise by unsuccessfully pulling the starter rather than by walking behind it as it mowed the grass.

There was a time, in Methodism, when all the ministers moved manse on the same day. No-one else in the country could move, as all the removal firms were signed up by the Methodists. A sort of ministerial musical manse, no doubt accompanied by several Wesleyan hymns!

Mark, St

The famous nudist in the Gospels who, when Jesus was arrested in the Garden of Gethsemane, is described like this: 'And there followed him a certain young man, having a linen cloth cast about his naked body. As the soldiers laid hold on him he left the linen cloth, and fled from them naked.'

Mark is the author of the second Gospel – which, scholars believe, was actually written first. In later life he is said to have become Bishop of Alexandria. When the Moslems conquered the Middle East, some merchants of Venice rescued his body by carrying it off and very cleverly shouting that the coffin was a crate of pork, which is unclean meat to Moslems.

In the Book of Common Prayer, the collect or special prayer which encourages people to read the scriptures says, 'Grant that we may Read, Mark, Learn and inwardly digest them' – which seems a little unfair on Matthew, Luke and John.

Martin, St

Martin is best remembered for cutting his cloak in two, giving half to warm a beggar on a cold winter's night. That night in a dream he saw Christ wearing the second half of his cloak – and was so affected that the next morning he was baptised.

Martin made his gift as an act of free generosity, but his bells apparently still feel they are owed five farthings. Londoners are apt to think of St Martin in the Fields, but he was actually Bishop of the City of Tours, on the River Loire in France.

A Scottish St Martin is that country's equivalent of the English St Swithin. If it rains on his day, 4 July, it will be wet for the next forty.

Matins (or Mattins)

A service of morning prayer found less and less in the Anglican Church where, in recent years, the emphasis has been on the Eucharist or communion service. Should you complain at being present at such a service, usually held mid-morning, spare a thought for medieval monks who would creep from their cells to a freezing cold chapel at either midnight or two in the morning to say this office. Anglican priests are required to say both Matins and Evensong each day.

Matrimony

Wedlock – or deadlock – depending on your point of view. Another word for marriage.

A vicar was conducting a double wedding, for two gypsy couples. At the end of the service, on their way out of church, one of the bridegrooms whispered to the priest, 'Excuse me, your reverence, but you've married the wrong couples.'

The priest, aghast, asked the bridegroom to stick around while he thought of a way out of this terrible predicament. As he stood agonising about whether a re-run of the ceremony was required, both bridegrooms came to him and one of them said, 'Not to worry, Vic, we've thought about it, and we think it best to leave things the way they are.'

Incidentally, you cannot normally be married other than between the hours of 8 am and 6 pm. Anyone has the right to be married in the parish church where they live.

If your friends ever threaten to object during the service when the priest asks if there are any reasons why these two 'should not be joined together in Holy Matrimony', try to dissuade them. Should they object, the service has to stop there and then while an enquiry is made into the matter.

Matthias, St

Chosen by lot by the eleven to be a disciple in place of the traitor Judas after the latter had hung himself and burst asunder. When all Judas's bowels gushed out, the lot fell upon Matthias. He was to suffer martyrdom when he was beheaded in Jerusalem by the Jews – which is why he is usually represented with a sword or an axe.

Methodists

Members of the Methodist Church, founded by John Wesley in the 18th century.

John Wesley was the 15th child of Samuel Wesley, Rector of Epworth in Lincolnshire. In 1738 he was converted by a reading of Luther's preface to the Epistle to the Romans, and set out on an evangelistic career which led him into conflict with the Church of England. He covered an average of 8,000 miles a year on horseback and established an annual conference of lay preachers.

Although Wesley wished to remain within the Church of England, an argument over ordaining bishops for work in America led to the independence of the Methodist movement from the Established Church.

Methodists are organised into circuits administered by a Superintendent; and districts over which a Chairman is appointed. The business of the Methodists is decided at Conference, at which policy and appointments are discussed.

Milk of Human Kindness

Vicar: Did you like my sermon on the Milk of Human Kindness?
Parishioner: Yes, but I wish it had been condensed.

Minister

A minister is a servant, and thus a prime minister, it is interesting to note, is a chief servant. The word 'minister' therefore reminds its holder of his obligation and duty to serve his fellow men.

The word 'deacon' also means a servant. In the Church of England a man is 'made deacon' when he first becomes a member of the clergy. He is then 'ordained priest' but as a priest he still remains a deacon, a servant. He can then be consecrated bishop, but as a bishop he still remains a priest and a deacon – a servant. In the Roman Catholic Church, he can finally become Pope, but he still remains a bishop, priest and deacon; and indeed one of the Pope's great titles is *servus servorum Dei* – the servant of the servants of God.

A minister in the church is involved in a great deal of administration, but that is all part of his servitude. As a servant of God he also quite often gives service to the people by giving them services.

Nowadays, there are also lay ministers who take services and assist in ministering to the congregation. These can be men or women. Women can be ministers (i.e. clergy) in the Nonconformist churches and deacons in the Church of England, but not priests or bishops.

Mission

Scene: a jungle clearing. A large iron pot is steaming over a blazing fire. Suddenly a pink sweaty face emerges through the steam. 'You can't boil me, I'm a friar,' gasps the missionary.

For hundreds of years, missionaries would leave this country to take Christianity to the heathen abroad. Now other countries are getting their own back. Fresh-faced Americans, smart-suited and polite to a fault, appear on our doorsteps and introduce us to the mysteries of Mormonism or the wonders of Christian Science.

Billy Graham keeps coming back to England to convert the masses to Christianity, while stay-at-home evangelists beam in their mission messages by satellite from America. Missionaries, from being boiled, roasted or on the defensive, are now on the attack!

MITRE

From the Greek world meaning 'a turban'. Mitres, however, are not turbans. Mitres are shaped like an upside-down shield, and can be found on the heads of bishops of Western churches, as distinct from bishops of the Eastern or Orthodox churches who wear metal crowns.

The mitre needs very careful tailoring to fit the bishop's skull, lest it be blown off by a sudden gust of wind during a procession and, contrary to the rumour spread by some comedians, does not conceal a pack of sandwiches for the journey.

The two strips of material which hang down at the rear of the mitre are called 'lappets', for no obvious reason.

The mitre is removed during prayers, and the main parts of the communion service. On removal from the episcopal head, it is vigorously handed to the bishop's chaplain, thus giving the chaplain something to do, a reason for being there. Woe to the chaplain who fails to catch it . . .

NARTHEX

Sounds vaguely cockney, but it's a sort of fenced-off piece of a Byzantine church, separated from the nave by pillars or a screen. It is occupied by people who are not baptised or confirmed.

Not to be confused with the 'exonarthex', which is a porch which opens onto the street.

NAVE

The long bit of the church building extending from the west end to the choir or chancel. Its name comes from the Latin word *navis,* meaning a ship.

If the church is cruciform (cross-shaped) in character, then the nave extends as far as the cross-pieces running north and south, usually called transepts. The nave is often separated from the chancel or choir by a screen in stone, metal or wood, and in many churches there are steps up from the nave to the chancel.

NEALE, JOHN MASON

Hymn-writer and priest who was presented to the living of Crawley in Sussex when it was an old village and not yet a new town. However, ill-health prevented his accepting and instead he spent the next three winters in Madeira. He was Warden of Sackville College, East Grinstead, for the last 20 years of his life until he died in 1866 at the age of 48.

Neale wrote his hymns and sermons not kneeling, but standing at a lectern. Over 60 of his translations appear in the English Hymnal, together with nine original works. The latter include *O Happy Band of Pilgrims; Christian, dost thou see them?* and *Jerusalem the Golden.* And also the hymn which begins:

> *Art thou weary, art thou languid,*
> *Art thou sore distrest?*

and ends

> *Angels, martyrs, prophets, virgins,*
> *Answer Yes!*

NEWMAN, JOHN HENRY

Newman was born in 1801, and lived for almost the whole of the 19th century. He had an evangelical upbringing, went up to Oxford in 1817 and became a fellow of Oriel eight years later. In 1828 he was appointed Vicar of St Mary's, the University Church, where he preached and then published what he called *Parochial and Plain Sermons.* At the same time he contributed to the *Tracts for the Times,* defending the Church of England as a *via media* between Rome and Protestantism. He became one of the leaders of the Oxford movement, but soon his worries and anxieties began. Little by little they increased until he moved out of Oxford to a village a few miles away called Littlemore. In 1843 he resigned the living of St Mary's and, living in Littlemore, preached in the village church a famous sermon on 'The Parting of Friends'. In 1845 he became a Roman Catholic.

His time as a Roman Catholic was beset by yet more anxieties and worries. He was ordained in Rome, worked in Birmingham and Dublin, and was then, on his return to England, involved in a tedious and rambling controversy with Cardinal Manning because of his critical review of a book by Manning in a periodical called *The Rambler.*

Newman then published his Apology for His Life, *Apologia Pro Vita Sua,* and wrote the *Dream of Gerontius,* later set to music by Sir

Edward Elgar. His famous hymns include ***Firmly I believe and truly, Praise to the Holiest in the Height*** and ***Lead Kindly Light***.

Cardinal Newman was made a cardinal in 1879 and died in 1890.

The story is told of the old Cardinal Newman standing at the gate of Littlemore Church late in his life, listening to the choir singing Evensong to Anglican chant, with tears pouring down his cheeks. He did much for the Church of England, and much too for Roman Catholicism in this country.

NEWTON, JOHN (1725-1807)

Forced to go to sea and engage in the infamous slave trade, Newton was converted to Christianity when he was 23. He left the sea and was appointed to the position of Surveyor of the Tides at Liverpool. He was ordained in 1764 and served as curate at Olney where he collaborated with William Cowper on the Olney Hymns, published in 1779.

Among his best-loved hymns are *Glorious Things of Thee are Spoken, Amazing Grace* and *How Sweet the Name of Jesus Sounds.*

Having been involved in the slave trade, he worked with William Wilberforce to bring about its abolition.

If a slave trader can be converted to Christianity, write such beautiful hymns and work to stamp out slavery, there's hope for everyone!

I went to Africa that I might be able to sin to my heart's content. I was a wild beast on the coast of Africa till the Lord caught and tamed me.

John Newton

NONCONFORMIST

Nowadays, a man who belongs to the Free Churches, but originally the name given to those in the 17th century who refused to conform to the discipline and practice of the Established Church in England, particularly in matters of ceremony.

It later came to refer to almost every Christian group which was not Anglican, Roman Catholic or Eastern Orthodox. The term 'Nonconformist' thus embraced Baptists, Congregationalists, Methodists, Presbyterians and Quakers.

The main difference to the outsider was that Anglicans, Roman Catholics and Orthodox congregations were liable to worship in church while the Nonconformists went to chapel. In some places you could eat sweets in chapel, but in others chapel was far stricter than church. While the Roman Catholics had a 'father' and the Anglicans a 'vicar', the Nonconformists were likely to be subjected to the lengthy sermons of a minister, an elder or a deacon.

Bedfordshire has always been a great breeder of Nonconformists. The most famous of these was the 17th-century John Bunyan, who was born at Elstow. He was imprisoned in Bedford Gaol and was the author of *Pilgrim's Progress.*

None

None, to rhyme with moan or groan, is the name of the last of the old monastic offices (or services). It is supposed to be recited at the ninth hour, which is actually 3 pm, but is in fact often said at noon, to rhyme with June and moon and spoon

Novice

A probationary member of a monastery or a convent: in other words, a monk or nun with L plates.

The novitiate (or novice time) usually lasts for a year, during which the novice can leave without penalty or disgrace – or can be asked to leave by the superior of the community. When a novice begins the probationary year, a ceremony of 'clothing' takes place, during which the novice puts on the habit of the community.

Nun

In the Bible Joshua was the son of Nun, which leads to unfortunate suggestions that either his parent did not exist or that she may have been a sister. However, in that case, as a mother she must have been superior.

Nuncio

A representative of the Holy See or Vatican who is accredited to a government and who acts in an ambassadorial or diplomatic capacity. In contrast to secular ambassadors, he is not generally required to lie abroad for the good of his Pope, though in former times he may have had to explain what a particular papal bull was doing at the Court of St James.

There was a time when the Nuncio collected tithes due to the Pope. Such tithes are no longer due and therefore cannot be collected, leaving the Nuncio plenty of time to attend great occasions, banquets and other diplomatic functions.

Nuptial Mass

A mass celebrated within the context of a marriage service, this practice is more often encountered within the Roman Catholic Church.

Some Church of England weddings encompass Communion, but it is then usually restricted to the bride and bridegroom.

Oberammergau

As a thank-you for the ending of the plague in 1633, the villagers of Oberammergau in Upper Bavaria vowed to enact a Passion Play every ten years. With one or two interruptions due to wars, the play has been performed ever since. Up to 700 villagers take some part in the production and presentation of the play. Characteristically, newspapers make play of any controversy surrounding the casting of Jesus, but you might expect that in a small community. It must surely be the only community where there is competition for crucifixion. Any small change in the production – a word changed, or a different emphasis – can be the cause of argument.

Occasional Offices

These are services in the Book of Common Prayer which are used only when occasion may demand.

They include such services as Baptism (either of Infants or of Those of Riper Years), Confirmation, Holy Matrimony, the Visitation of the Sick, the Communion of the Sick, the Burial of the Dead, and the Commination.

The last-named is never used today as occasion never demands it. Thank God for occasion! It was composed for use on Ash Wednesday, includes the solemn recitation of curses and its cheerful and encouraging sub-title is 'Denouncing of God's anger and judgements against sinners'.

Offertory

The offering of the bread and wine (and water) to be consecrated at the Eucharist. Nowadays, these are usually brought up to the altar from the body of the church by two or three members of the congregation in procession.

The offertory can also refer to the money which has been collected by the sidesmen, also called the collection.

Office

The Office, or The Divine Office, is the name given to those services which priests are obliged to say daily.

The traditional monastic offices are Matins, Lauds, Prime, Terce, Sext, None, Vespers and Compline. These eight offices (consisting of psalms, hymns, lessons and prayers) are still used by the Roman Catholic Church.

At the Reformation, the Church of England produced from the old eight the two offices of Morning and Evening Prayer, Matins (or Mattins) and Evensong. It is the clergy's duty to recite these offices

daily, and in many parishes the parish priest valiantly rings the church bell to announce to the people that he is doing so.

The Roman Catholic offices can all be found in a book called the Breviary (pronounced Breeviary). In 1911 the length of the offices was considerably shortened and so the Breviary became even briefer.

In 1980 the Church of England produced its Alternative Service Book and its offices too became somewhat shorter, although the ASB itself was very much fatter than the Book of Common Prayer. The Prayer Book usually had at the most just over 700 pages but the ASB easily triumphed over this, weighing in at 1,292.

Og

Og was King of Bashan, a giant, and very old and wicked indeed. He was so old, according to Hebrew legend, that he dated from before the Flood, and had survived by climbing on the roof of the Ark.

Og is chiefly remembered for the size of his bedstead which, the Book of Deuteronomy in the Bible tells us, measured nine cubits long by four cubits wide.

He met his Waterloo, so to speak, when he was unwise enough to take on Moses when that remarkable gentleman was leading the Children of Israel to their Promised Land. Og tried to pick up a complete mountain to hurl at them – but became so tangled up in it that Moses was able to step in with a nifty jab to an unprotected part of his anatomy and finish him off. Still, the memory remained strong. So it's easy to imagine that Og was the giant with whom small children in Bashan would have been threatened by exasperated parents: 'Shut it, Reuben, or I'll send for Og!'

Nowadays parents, forgetting Og and his iron bedstead, have been heard to cry, 'One more word, Wayne, and I'll get the vicar.'

The Church is an anvil that has worn out many hammers.

English proverb

Oratorio

A piece of sacred music, with religious text but without dramatic presentation, scenery or costume. It was a Bishop of London who objected to Biblical representations on stage. What would he have made of the mystery play enacted on a cart? Examples are Handel's *Messiah* and *Solomon,* Elgar's *Dream of Gerontius,* Stainer's *Crucifixion,* and Mendelssohn's *Elijah.*

Handel's *Messiah* was first performed in 1742, and is now a regular feature of choral society repertoires, especially in the North of England. Many churches organise a 'bring it and sing it' event, to which enthusiastic amateur singers repair with the score – and the hope that everyone else knows it better than they do.

Orders

Orders are orders and like She, they must be obeyed. There are three Orders in the Church – bishops, priests and deacons. And, at ordinations, men are made deacon, ordained priest, and consecrated bishop.

At the consecration of an African bishop, when the time came for all the other bishops to gather round and lay their hands on his head, a visitor enquired, 'What are they doing to him now?'

'Ah!' said his friend. 'They are removing his back-bone.'

Organ

Organs in church date back to the eighth century. Their use in church was opposed by the Puritans and in 1644 they were banned from churches – and in many cases destroyed.

Organs are expensive beasts to keep. They require regular attention and cleaning. They are touchy about humidity and temperature. Both organs and organists need very careful handling. Cross the organist, and suddenly there's no music in church on Sunday. Those contemplating Holy Matrimony should be sure to get the organist on their side early on and take advice before asking him to play *A Whiter Shade of Pale* or the Clog Dance from *Hansel and Gretel*. Organists are in short supply, possibly because they are constantly tempted to play for wealthier congregations somewhere in Scandinavia, if advertisements in the church press are any guide.

Organists are key people who can make or break worship. To cope with some choirs, they will need nerves of steel, the patience of Job, and the cunning of a serpent. Musicianship is helpful, too. Some are

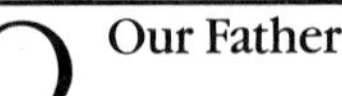

paid, others are not. Some have to earn their living, others don't. The Royal College of Organists is there to maintain standards and encourage excellence, and cathedral and University college organists are usually the highest flyers of the lot. Organists are sometimes Choirmasters, or Masters of the Music, but not invariably so.

At one boarding school, the headmaster installed a blower for the chapel organ, perhaps despairing of students staying awake long enough to pump enough air through the bellows. The blower was a cylinder vacuum cleaner, blowing air from the locker room below the chapel. Careful plans were laid to reconnect the pipe to the 'suck' end of the cylinder. Conspirators imagined sheet music, the notes, the dust – even the very vitals of the beast – being drawn down from the chapel and sprayed into the locker room. The plot was discovered and thwarted.

Our Father

A theological student got half way through the Lord's Prayer in the middle of a hospital ward service and then his mind went a complete blank. In a sudden rush of inspiration he ad-libbed to the patients, 'I bet one of you knows how this continues . . .'

Mercifully, because of their religious education in school, or being taught the words at their mothers' knee, one or two of them picked up the words and ran with them right to the *Amen* at the end.

There are a number of corruptions of the prayer. One begins: 'Our Father who art in Hendon, Harrow be they name. Thy Kingston come, thy Wimbledon. Give us this day our daily Brent.'

A small child, impatient to jump into bed, was heard to say, 'Dear God, same as last night, Amen.'

As men's prayers are a disease of the will so are their creeds a disease of the intellect.

Ralph Waldo Emerson

Parish

Wherever you go in England, you can't escape the parish, be it civil or ecclesiastical. Thus, every unmarried woman can be called 'a spinster of this parish'.

The parish is an area to which priests or ministers are appointed. Their job is to be responsible for the pastoral care of everyone in the area – a care (or cure) shared with, and delegated by, the bishop of the diocese.

The parish may date from pre-Christian times when a landowner was under a duty to provide a priest for the people on his land, to lead the worship, carry out sacrifices and cast spells. Today, priests are expected to be similarly omni-competent. They must be good preachers, tireless visitors of both the sick and the healthy, know how to deal with poltergeists, raise money for decaying buildings, instruct the young and care for the old and everyone in between!

Parishes are the baseline communities in the church structure, being themselves grouped into deaneries which, in their turn, are subdivisions of the diocese. Roman Catholics also have parishes, usually larger than Anglican parishes, due to the high cost of building churches.

Ecclesiastical parishes are not to be confused with the civil parishes into which Britain is divided, which all have their own registers of electors, elected councils with limited financial powers, and which form the lowest tier of local government.

Parish Magazines

It has been estimated that these are the greatest potential for good or ill in the land. One priest said he always tore up any parish magazines he found because of the harm they might do. Hard to think they could do any harm when the vicar's letter begins: 'Well, here we are again at the start of another new year.'

Some are more newsy than that introduction suggests – what's actually been going on amongst the wives? And what is the Men's Society *really* doing behind closed doors on the second Monday in the month (except in April and August)?

Where else would you find gardening tips, an appreciation of the oldest bellringer in the village, secrets of the vicarage kitchen, a parish directory of all the key people, times of doctors' surgeries and duty chemists, and the readings from the 10 o'clock Eucharist?

Patrick, St

St Patrick led an eventful life from AD 389 until AD 461. At the age of sixteen he was captured by raiders and taken to Ireland as a slave, where he looked after pigs for about six years. He then ran away, begged a passage on a ship and escaped. The crew weren't keen. 'Another mouth to feed,' they cried. Nevertheless they took him on board – and then they ran out of food. Patrick, however, had a nose for swine. He prayed, guided the boat to land and led the crew to a conveniently-situated herd, thus saving their bacon.

Convinced that he should convert the Irish, Patrick studied in a monastery at Lerins, an island in the Mediterranean. From there he went to Auxerre where he was ordained.

Later he was sent to Ireland where he was consecrated bishop, and tried to convert his former master who, enraged at the thought of having to submit to his former slave, set his house and belongings on fire – and hurled himself into the flames. He went to the court of the High King Laoghaire (pronounced Leary) and converted several members of the royal family, giving point to the place name Dun Laoghaire. He was opposed by the Druids, who were not into competition. The famous hymn, ***St Patrick's Breastplate,*** is believed to have been a catalogue of powerful prayers aimed at the Druids and their spells.

Patrick was responsible for converting many of the Irish, for organising the church in Ireland and linking it more closely to the church in Europe. In popular mythology he is also credited with ridding Ireland of snakes. 'Go', he roared, and they did, being obedient serpents. They haven't been back since.

Paul, St

'Oh, no! Not another letter from Paul,' the early Christians used to cry when the postman delivered the mail. Paul was one of the world's most famous writers of letters. He was forever encouraging women to wear hats and keep quiet.

In his early days he was called Saul, but on the road to Damascus he saw the light and had a change of life. He became Paul, gave up persecuting Christians and became a missionary instead. He set off on his Far Trek 1, Far Trek 2 and Far Trek 3, like a Captain of the Ancient Kirk – in the words of the 20th-century split infinitive, to boldly go where no (Christian) man had gone before.

The worst moment for the atheist is when he is really thankful and has nobody to thank.

Dante Gabriel Rossetti

Peter, St

Chief of the Apostles, likened by Jesus to a rock, which is what the name means. However, when Jesus was arrested, things became too hot for poor Peter who got cold feet and denied Him three times before the cock crew. Peter panicked then, but later grew up to become one of the greatest heroes of the Church.

'Thou art Peter, and upon this rock I will build my church', Christ said to him. 'I will give unto thee the keys of the Kingdom of Heaven' – which is why Peter is always seen with a pair of jumbo-sized keys.

He was to end his earthly life crucified upside down – at his own request, as he did not consider himself worthy to die in the same manner as his Master.

Pharisees

People in the New Testament who took themselves very seriously. Nowadays they can still be found in Church, Parliament and Press, bewailing other people's sins.

The word 'pharisee' comes from the Hebrew for 'the separate ones', a Jewish religious party who claimed to be above worldly things . . .

Philemon

The easily-missed shortest book of the Bible is a missive about a missing slave. It consists of only 25 verses – in three of which St Paul insists on mentioning his bowels and their need to be refreshed.

When God gives us bread, men will supply the butter.
Yiddish proverb

Philip, St

One of the twelve disciples. His day is 1 May, when he is remembered with St James. Together they are affectionately known as 'Pip and Jim'.

The name Philip really means 'lover of horses', but you'll usually spot him in medieval illustrations with a basket of loaves and fishes – a reference to his close involvement in the story of Christ's feeding of the five thousand.

Photographers

The real heroes on any wedding day.

Who could fail to admire their agility as they teeter from the back of one pew to another, their cheek when they ask the vicar before the service what he will or won't permit? Whereupon they then disregard every sanction, every request not to use a flashgun during the exchanging of the rings.

Who could not be impressed by their endless flow of inane cajoling banter as they strive, against overwhelming odds, to marshal the aunts, uncles, irritable page boys, sulking bridesmaids . . . 'Can we have just the family now? What am I saying? Both families . . . Cheer up, you don't have to talk to each other again until the christening . . . No, I jest.'

Piscina

An arched niche in the south wall of the sanctuary in a church. It's a holy sink with a shelf for the cruets and a drainhole which connects with the ground below the wall, so that the washing-up water can run away.

What washing-up? During the communion service the priest washes his hands by having water poured over them. After the communion, the chalice (cup) and paten (plate) are washed carefully so no trace of bread and wine remains on them. Since the water is consecrated by contact with the bread and wine, it must flow into consecrated ground – hence the drain set directly into the foundations.

The priest is often assisted at these ablutions by an altar boy or server.

Polycarp, St

Not a fishy lady, but one of the early martyrs of the church. Polycarp was one of those hardy souls who, when Roman emperors were killing Christians with the enthusiasm usually reserved for swatting flies, flatly refused to deny his beliefs and sacrifice to idols. He was tied to a stake to be burned – but, as the tale goes, the flames refused to touch him. So the emperor's men had to kill him with a dagger.

Pope

A word derived from both Greek and Roman words meaning 'father'. Once used as a title of any bishop in the Western Church, and still used of a priest in the Orthodox Church, it is now generally taken to refer to the Bishop of Rome.

Pope John XXIII was perhaps the most-loved modern Pope. Elected at the age of 77, he opened the doors and windows of the Roman Catholic Church to let fresh air in and some of the stuffiness out. For him, the whole world was his family, and his reforms led to Roman Catholics worshipping in their own languages rather than in Latin.

The present Pope, John Paul II, has probably travelled further than any other Pope in history – and, to his credit, can at least be relied on to know what country he is visiting, unlike certain temporal Heads of State.

The history of the Papacy itself has been a chequered and sometimes bloody one. But amongst the volumes of stories told about it, perhaps the most curious one concerns Pope Joan, a woman who passed herself off as a man and – according to a chronicle written in about 1250 – was elected Pope and given the title of John VIII. She reigned for two years from 855, her reign coming to an end when she gave birth to a child and died. This is only one of the versions about her – and all of them are dismissed by serious scholars as pure (or impure) invention.

The only Englishman ever to occupy the papal throne was Nicholas Breakspear, who reigned as Adrian IV for just five years in the middle of the 12th century.

Prayer

Talking to God and listening to Him. Prayers can be long or short, silent or loud, in everyday language or the traditional words of the church. The shortest prayers simply evoke the name of the Deity – as in 'Oh God' or 'Oh my God'. Prayer has been described as 'The Church's Banquet' (George Herbert), and prayers before meals are called Grace. Some graces can be amazing.

Prayers can be said anywhere at any time, although Miguel Cervantes declared that 'a leap over the hedge is better than good men's prayers'.

Pontius Pilate

Roman Governor at the time of the Crucifixion of Jesus. Sometimes portrayed by children as sitting in an aeroplane . . . Pontius the Pilot. Get it?

England has two books, the Bible and Shakespeare.
England made Shakespeare but the Bible made England.
Victor Hugo

Presbyter

An elder of the church. The early church modelled its organisation on the Jewish synagogue, where authority resided in the company of elders. There is some debate as to whether a Presbyter is the equivalent of a bishop. Some sources believe that a bishop or overseer is the equivalent of the chairman of group of elders.

Presbyterian

A member of the Presbyterian Church, a church governed by presbyters. The Church of Scotland is the only State Church which is presbyterian. A little-known fact is that the Moderator of the Church of Scotland is the only person to have the royal crown emblazoned on the buttons of a religious garment, in his case his frock coat!

The Presbyterian Church is governed at ground level by the minister and the elders, then by presbyteries made up of local presbyters or elders and ministers over a defined geographical area. The next layer is the synod, and the supreme governing body is the General Assembly made up of equal numbers of elders and ministers. There are slightly fewer than one and a half million Presbyterians in the United Kingdom.

Presbytery

A bunch of representative elders and ministers of the Presbyterian Church meeting together. Oddly enough, it is also a dwelling for a Roman Catholic priest or priests with or without a housekeeper. More confusing still, a Presbyterian minister doesn't live in a presbytery, but in a manse. He is not, however, a Methodist minister just because he lives, like them, in a manse.

A Presbyterian minister in Hawick was no mean cellist. He was practising one Sunday when a knock on the manse door revealed a group of elders, all with long stern faces.

'Ye'll no be playing your instrument on the Lord's day, Minister,' they said menacingly before leaving.

It was less a question than a statement. The cello was put away.

Love thy neighbour, even when he plays the trombone.
Jewish proverb

Provost

Not a military policeman but the Dean of certain cathedrals, usually those less ancient cathedrals which were formerly parish churches. There are, for example, provosts of the cathedrals of Birmingham, Blackburn, Bradford, Chelmsford, Derby, Leicester, Newcastle, Portsmouth, Sheffield and Wakefield, but deans of Canterbury, Chester, Chichester, Durham, Ely, Exeter, Gloucester, Lichfield, Lincoln, Norwich, St Albans, Salisbury, Wells, Winchester and York.

Psalms

The hymns of the Jews and some of the greatest religious poems in the world. Numbering 150, they are known as the Psalms of David, but they weren't, of course, written by King David himself.

The most famous is Psalm 23, *The Lord is my Shepherd;* the longest is Psalm 119 with 176 verses; the shortest – with two – is Psalm 117.

The Psalms talk of the activity and nature of God who is Creator, King, Saviour, Judge; and God who is holy, loving and faithful.

In the Book of Common Prayer the psalms are so divided as to be said in order once each month. Two or three psalms are set for each of the 30 mornings and evenings. The longest evening is the 15th for which Psalm 78 with 73 verses is set.

On the following morning, the 16th, the first psalm of the day was once particularly appropriate on the morning following a General Election. The opposition party had won during the night and the next day the Psalm began, 'O God the heathen are come into thine inheritance.'

The singing of psalms in the Church of England is usually to Anglican Chant, but many hymns have been based on psalms. Examples are *As Pants the Hart, All People that on Earth Do Dwell* (Psalm 100) and *O God our Help in Ages Past.*

If great poetry is the essential heart of the language of the psalms there are some charming vagaries. Clearly when Adam covered up a crucial part of himself, he didn't go far enough, for Psalm 147 states that God 'Neither delighteth . . . in any man's legs.'

Horses are not very much liked in the psalms – witness, 'Be ye not like to horse and mule, which have no understanding' (Psalm 32); 'A horse is counted but a vain thing to save a man' (Psalm33); and 'he hath no pleasure in the strength of an horse' (Psalm 147).

Meanwhile, in Psalm 89 there appears to have been some disturbance in a suburban garden – if 'Thou hast overthrown all his hedges' is anything to go by. And in Psalm 144 the writer makes the extraordinary plea that 'our sheep may bring forth thousands and ten thousands in our streets.' He then proceeds to say that this would ensure that there would be 'no complaining in our streets' and 'Happy are the people that are in such a case.' One wonders what they would think of that in Acacia Avenue or Laburnum Grove?

Pulpit

From the Latin word for a platform, this is the place from where the sermon is preached in church. Pulpits vary enormously in size and style, being fashioned from wood, stone or metal.

Visiting preachers should always inspect the pulpit to discover where the light switch is, how to switch on the microphone if there is one, where the trapdoor is should a quick exit be needed after an unpopular sermon.

One pulpit in Arlington, Texas, has an array of switches, controls and dimmers – indeed it is as well-equipped as a theatre. One wrong switch and the whole congregation may start revolving!

Magdalen College, Oxford, has an outdoor pulpit . . . unusual, given the English climate.

In many Nonconformist churches, the size of the pulpit reflects the emphasis and value given to preaching in their tradition. Moving sermons have been delivered by early Methodists on horseback.

Many clergy are chary of preaching from pulpits, preferring to preach at ground-level rather than from six feet above contradiction. They may, however, be neglecting an important insight. Preachers need to be heard and seen, if not to be believed, then at least to exist.

Queen Anne's Bounty

Not some royal confectionery, but a fund set up by the Queen in 1704, to funnel parish revenues confiscated by Henry VIII back to the poorer clergy and parishes. It was later used for the building and repair of clergy houses. The fund attracted grants from Parliament and private legacies and, in 1948, was united with the Ecclesiastical Commissioners to form the Church Commissioners for England. This new body was charged with the management of the financial and property resources of the Church of England.

Quo Vadis?

A novel by the Polish writer Henrÿ Senkiewicz which has been three times filmed – in 1912, 1924 and 1951. It tells of a Roman general, a foreign queen, a giant slave, the Emperor Nero and Saints Peter and Paul. Christians are thrown to the lions, Nero (Emil Jannings in 1924, Peter Ustinov in 1951) fiddles while Rome burns and crowds of extras loudly cheer and jeer from their seats in the arena. At least, they were loud in 1951. The films of 1912 and 1924 were silent.

'Quo vadis?' itself means 'Whither goest thou?' and was a question put by the risen Christ to the Apostle Peter on the road, as he was fleeing from persecution in Rome. Peter immediatelty turned back to the city – and to his death.

Rabbi

A Jewish religious leader or teacher. Jesus was called 'Rabbi' by his friends.

Of all religious people, rabbis tell the best jokes and the best stories. Rabbi Lionel Blue tells this one, among many others.

Two women were on safari when suddenly a gorilla leapt out at them, grabbed one of them, embraced her and carried her off to his lair. There he embraced her some more. The other woman escaped and later visited her bandaged friend in hospital. 'How do you feel?' she asked.

'All this time and not a word, not even some fruit!' came the reply.

There is no pillow so soft as a clear conscience.
French proverb

Rahab

The kind-hearted prostitute of Jericho who sheltered two Jewish spies sent by Joshua, the son of Nun, to report on the military installations. However, someone spilt the beans to the king of Jericho who sent the police round to Rahab's house.

'Evening, Rahab,' they said, flexing their knees. 'Hand over those Jewish spies ... we know you've got them hidden there.'

Rahab, no slouch, replied, 'Sergeant, there've been men in and out of here all night. You don't expect me to know where they've come from, surely. Mind you, there were two men here but they left just as they were closing the city gates. If you get a move on, I'm sure you'll catch them.'

The police left in hot pursuit, camels, blue lights, the works.

Rahab had hidden the spies on the roof where she struck a bargain with them. 'If you promise to spare me and my family, I'll not split on you to the fuzz.' They readily agreed – no Jewish spy in his right mind fancied a year in Jericho's nick – and arranged for Rahab to identify her house with a scarlet thread in the window. Everyone inside the house would be saved.

When Jericho fell, Rahab and all her family were the sole survivors because of her kindness in hiding the Jewish spies.

The scarlet thread may be the precursor of the red light that indicates where big-hearted harlots are to be found . . .

Ramsey, Arthur Michael

The hundredth Archbishop of Canterbury, who died in 1988. Described as 'a genial Friar Tuck of a man.' A great pastor and teacher, he looked like everybody's favourite grandfather, with twinkling eyes and bushy eyebrows. He had previously been Bishop of Durham and Archbishop of York.

Red Hat

A large red, broad-brimmed hat with two clusters of fifteen tassels given to a cardinal after his appointment by the Pope.

Being a rather impractical piece of headgear, the hat is never worn again. It might cause small boys to laugh irreverently, or be blown away by gusts of theological controversy sweeping around the Vatican.

At the cardinal's death, his red hat is suspended over his tomb – presumably ready for him to rise from the dead, put it on and wear in heaven, where no winds blow and small boys know better than to laugh at a cardinal.

Red Sea

Where the Egyptians got their feet very wet and died in great numbers as they pursued the escaping Israelites.

God had caused a great wind to blow, piling up the waters on either side as the Israelites crossed on dry ground. Once they were safely across, the waters rolled back – engulfing the whole Egyptian army, their horses, chariots, cavalry and infantry. The Israelites looked back on this miracle with great wonder and thanksgiving – not least because the night before they left Egypt they had borrowed heavily from the Egyptians, and now had no need to repay the loan.

We don't know whether Moses whistled for the wind to blow the waters back: if he did, it might explain why deep-sea fishermen carefully avoid whistling while at sea, lest the wind should come and make life even more uncomfortable for them.

Man is what he believes.
Anton Chekhov

Relic

This is part of a holy person's body or belongings kept after his death as a souvenir or memento or object of reverence. In the Topkapi Museum in Istanbul, for example, one is invited to view the right hand and the skull of St John the Baptist – but you'll have to go to Amiens Cathedral in Northern France to see his face . . . or at least, the front part of the skull, missing from the Topkapi exhibit.

The small village of Trimingham, in north Norfolk, prides itself on a church uniquely dedicated to The Head of John the Baptist. It dates from a con trick, maintained over many decades in late medieval times by wily priests, who attracted droves of pilgrims and, of course, very useful income, by maintaining that they had the holy head. What they in fact had was an alabaster cast bought for pence from Nottingham or Burton-on-Trent, where they were turned out by the dozen in Derbyshire-mined alabaster!

In the Middle Ages, as this story illustrates, relics were enormously popular and parts of the bodies of various saints could be found all over Europe. Indeed, any one saint or martyr might easily discover that the fourth finger of his right hand was simultaneously being venerated in churches in France and Italy and Spain. Nothing was too small for such devotion.

In a certain village in England where the church is dedicated to St John the Baptist, the headmaster of the local church school has been rung up by parents asking 'Can I speak to the Headof John the Baptist, please?'

Religious Affairs

Not necessarily of the 'Vicar's showgirl lovenest in belfry' variety.

Almost anything falls within this category, which is why the BBC have employed religious affairs correspondents to work in radio. If issues can be commented upon by sociologists, trades union spokespeople, economists and sundry political pundits, why not by someone with a religious perspective?

Douglas Brown was probably the first specialist correspondent appointed by the BBC, followed by Gerald Priestland whose series *Priestland's Progress* brought a postbag of over 20,000 letters. Priestland was also responsible for *Yours Faithfully,* short Saturday-morning pieces on Radio 4, one of which was about the sex life of American frogs. His secretary spent evenings dancing in West End shows like the *The Best Little Whorehouse in Texas,* – another way of looking at religious affairs.

No man can break any of the Ten Commandments, he can only break himself against them.

G K Chesterton

Requiem

'Requiem' is the Latin for 'rest', the first word of the introit of the Mass celebrated for the dead: *Requiem aeternam dona eis Domine* (Rest eternal grant him, O Lord). The words for the requiem have inspired some of the most sublime music of the Christian Church, from early traditional plainsong to wonderfully elaborate versions which suggest the concert hall rather then the church – Verdi's *Requiem* is a particular example. When Delius wrote an alternative requiem, to words by Nietzsche, it caused a storm and was branded as 'pagan'.

One of the great modern examples is Benjamin Britten's *War Requiem,* combining Latin text with anti-war poems by Wilfred Owen.

Requiem is also a musical piece by Andrew Lloyd Webber, written after *Cats* and *Starlight Express,* but before *The Phantom of the Opera.* Of all the composers who have written music to the same words none have inspired such a blaze of publicity.

Reredos

A word to know when touring churches, as it's often uttered by guides in the confident expectation that everyone else present will understand. It's any kind of decoration to be found behind an altar. Earliest forms were painted on the wall; others have been carved in stone or wood, or worked in metal. They could be encrusted with jewels, decorated with statuary and devotional texts of an improving nature.

An artist looking at the blank back wall of a new church on a housing estate offered to paint a triptych – a three-panelled altar piece – to hang behind the altar. The church council agreed, and the artist worked on and off for a year to paint the panels. He worked in a shed in an apple orchard. Every so often he would stagger out of the shed, prop the panel he was working on against a tree and look at it from a distance.

'My neighbours thought I was mad,' he said later, 'dashing in and out of the shed with these large paintings.'

Eventually, the work was finished and the panels put in place in the church – a brilliant modern reredos. While working on the panels, showing Christ on the Cross, he had to think so much about what he was painting that he asked to be prepared for confirmation.

Resurrection

The Resurrection of Jesus on the first Easter Day lies at the heart of the Christian faith. Christians believe in the risen Christ as their living Lord. They believe, too, in the Life of the World to Come and the Resurrection of the Body.

At Windsor, a few years ago, a new graveyard was opened 'as a result of consultations with the bodies concerned.'

Retreat

Time spent in silence, prayer and meditation, away from the usual madness of everyday life.

The Gospels tell of the time Jesus spent in the wilderness after his baptism and there are instances of his withdrawing from his friends to be alone to pray.

Retreats are led by retreat conductors, priests or lay people with training and experience. While retreats may be spent in silence, other elements – music, dance, literature – are used to enrich the process. There are many retreat houses with a full and varied programme, and a growing interest in retreats is spanning the different Christian traditions and divides.

Rite

A rite is a form of service or worship. For example, in the Alternative Service Book or ASB there are two forms or rites for the Communion Service: Rite A and Rite B. Since they are different, it's important that worshippers know that they have the right rite in front of them.

The Roman Catholics were in great danger of using the wrong rites, so Pope Sixtus the Fifth established the Congregation of Sacred Rites in 1588 to make sure that the right rites were used throughout the Church.

Rochet

A white linen article of clothing worn by bishops, it's related to the surplice, though not as common. The rochet has sleeves which in the 18th century were excessively full, giving rise to the suspicion that it had been designed as an early life-jacket for seagoing prelates. It is worn beneath a chimere, the black sleeveless tunic worn by bishops.

Notice how these worthies have clothing and accessories with a language all their own – chimeres, rochets, mitres, crosiers, pectoral crosses. New bishops usually have to have all these mysteries explained to them with due deference by ecclesiastical outfitters who not only have a language all their own too, but an inventory that almost defies description.

To be a bishop is much, to deserve to be one is more.
St Jerome

Roman Catholic

The English branch of the Roman Catholic Church is very Irish but, whether Irish or English – or from any other part of the world – the people remain very faithful and in all parts of the world the masses continue to come to Mass.

The head of the Roman Catholic Church in England is the Cardinal Archbishop of Westminster. Westminster Cathedral is the Roman Catholic mother church, and is just down Victoria Street (named after a gracious Queen and mother) from the Anglican Westminster Abbey which is dedicated to St Peter.

There are two cathedrals (Anglican and Roman Catholic) in a number of English cities, Liverpool being just one example. There the Roman Catholic building, 'Paddy's Wigwam', or more properly 'The Cathedral of Christ the King,' and the Anglican edifice stand at either end of appropriately-named Hope Street.

Roman Catholic priests are always unmarried men but they are nevertheless normally addressed as 'Father'.

Royal Peculiar

St George's Chapel, Windsor, is known as a Royal Peculiar – and not because it is used for such things as ceremonies involving garters . . . In fact, it is not the only Royal Peculiar – Westminster Abbey is one too.

What this means is that the two establishments are akin to cathedrals in all particulars – except that they are independent of the authority of the Church of England as a whole, and responsible only to the Sovereign. The category was invented by Elizabeth I, as a sure way of keeping the belligerent abbey under control.

Sacristan

Similar to a virger or verger, but while a verger's room is a vestry a sacristan can be found in a sacristy. A sacristan's principal duty is to care for the sacred vessels. These are not holy boats, but the chalice and other vessels used at Holy Communion. The word is a direct descendant of the medieval Latin, ***sacristanus*** – which means, strangely enough, 'one in charge of sacred vessels'.

Saints

An apparently endless number of people who are forever going marching in at jazz concerts and football matches.

Most of them are dead clergymen, virgins or martyrs. Noteworthy amongst sainted men are Crispin and Crispinian, the patron saints of cobblers; Nicholas of pawnbrokers; Francis of animals; and David of the Welsh.

Among the famous women are St Catherine with her wheel; St Joan with her voices; St Cecilia with her music; St Monica, the mother of St Augustine ('Lord make me chaste, but not yet') of Hippo; and St Anne, the mother of Our Lady. St Mary herself has more English churches dedicated to her than any other saint. Indeed, there are sometimes two in the same town, as at Cambridge where Great St Mary's and Little St Mary's both continue to draw the crowds.

Among the lesser-known women is the brave Uncumber, or 'Wilgefortis' as she is sometimes named. She was a bearded virgin martyr who grew her beard to protect her virtue – frightening half to death some wretched man who approached her bed only to have the lower half of her face revealed to him from beneath the sheets. Since her father had sent the man, he was understandably upset – but over-reacted a bit by having the poor girl crucified, beard and all. Strange to say, she has not been remembered in any official calendar of the Church for many centuries. Less well known are the Apostles, famous for their spoons, St Pancras for his trains, St Vitus for his dance, St Michael for his underwear, St Leonard for his seaside resort, and St Bernard for rescuing stranded Alpine climbers with his cask of brandy round his neck.

It is better to be faithful than famous.
Theodore Roosevelt

Samson

Old Testament character who goes from bad to worse. As he grows up he sees one of the daughters of the Philistines and says to his mother and father, without any preamble, 'Get her for me'. When they gently expostulate, he simply repeats in the same charming manner, 'Get her for me.'

His wife weeps, but off he marches to a neighbouring town, kills 30 men, steals their belts and gives their clothes to 30 of his friends. After that he calmly announces that now he will do some real harm. He catches 300 foxes, ties them tail to tail, and fastens a firebrand between each pair. Then, when he has set the brands alight, he turns the foxes loose and drives them into the standing corn.

Verse follows verse in which he is either threatening slaughter or killing people. 'He smote them hip and thigh' we read. His wife in the meantime very wisely goes off to live with his best man.

He is perhaps one of the most unattractive characters in the whole Old Testament – a long-haired bully, violent and vindictive. Even when his new woman, Delilah, grabbed her scissors and cut off his hair, he managed to pull down the two pillars of the Temple. As the building came crashing to the ground he died and, by his death, killed even more people than those he'd managed to slay in his life. A hair-raising tale indeed.

SAUL

Saul was an Old Testament king, the father of Jonathan who loved David with a love surpassing the love of women.

There is a passage in the First Book of Samuel in which Saul goes into a cave to answer a call of nature. This is wonderfully rendered in a modern American version as 'Saul went into the cave to use the bathroom.'

SERVER

Until recently, a man or boy who assisted at the Communion service, moving the altar book from one side of the altar to the other, bringing bread and wine to the altar and generally assisting the priest or minister.

There has been a controversy over whether girls or women should be servers and, though a fierce rearguard action was fought by those who thought not, servers of both sexes are now to be found in church.

Christianity has died many times and risen again,
for it had a god who knew the way out of the grave.
G K Chesterton

SEX

Not to be confused with sext. Religion has always been an uneasy bedfellow with sex – people often think that sex is evil, something to be hidden away, not discussed, and certainly not celebrated. Generations of believers have suffered from this repression of what is, after all, one of God's gifts.

Spike Milligan tells the story of how, when he was growing up, he met a Jesuit priest in Rangoon and asked him whether he thought about women. 'All the time,' the priest replied. Milligan, who hadn't yet been told anything about sex by his parents, found that reply tremendously liberating.

The Puritans frowned on dancing and may well have made love while reading the Scriptures to avoid falling into temptation. Presumably they carefully avoided the Song of Solomon in the Old Testament, that glorious piece of writing celebrating physical love and ecstasy.

Sext

Not to be confused with sex. Priests and members of religious orders within the Roman Catholic Church are required to read prayers and portions of Scripture at particular times of the day. Sext is the series of prayers and readings to be recited at noon, the sixth hour of the day – thus, *sextus.*

Sheep

Animals forever cropping up in the Bible, wandering about and getting lost – flocks of them are watched by night in a well-known Christmas carol.

The story is told of a Roman Catholic bishop at a confirmation in Ireland asking the children about 'Feed my sheep, feed my lambs.'

'Who are the lambs?' he enquired.

'The laity,' answered the children.

'Very good,' he said. 'And who are the sheep?'

'The clergy,' they replied.

'Very good,' he said. 'And in the story of the Good Shepherd, who then am I?'

There was a deathly silence until one child stuck up his hand and replied, 'You, my Lord Bishop, are the Ram.'

Sienna, St Catherine of

Although she was around a bit too early to see the box for herself, having lived a life of notable saintliness and virtue in 14th century Italy, Catherine has, curiously, been adopted as the patron saint of television. Could it be because she had prophetic vision?

Simeon Stylites

Not the patron saint of ballpoint pens, but a holy man who lived in Antioch. At the age of about 26, he felt moved to build a pillar on which to spend the rest of his days in adoration and contemplation of God. Until he got used to the idea, he sat on quite a low pillar, but as his confidence grew, he built it to a height of forty cubits – about 46 feet – and, according to one version of the story, he remained there until his death.

Another story is that the post was simply a means of getting closer to God and that, to begin with, all the people below were very impressed. But then, as people will, they lost interest. Word reached Simeon that there was someone in the town who was even more saintly than him: a clown called Cornelius.

Simeon looked down from his perch one day and saw Cornelius entertaining some urchins with his juggling and his jokes. Intrigued, the saint decided to come down from his pole and find out more. He was told that once upon a time Cornelius had sold a grand and splendid suit of clothes to settle the debt of a widow, and that he continued to maintain her family. Others told how he spent all his takings on looking after an old man, on the point of death and living alone. Simeon was so impressed by this example of practical Christianity that he gave up pole-squatting and followed the example of Cornelius the Clown.

The heron's a saint when there are no fish in sight.
Bengali proverb

Sin

People say the worst sin of all is to be found out, but that's a cynical view of sin.

John Wesley said, 'Be ashamed of nothing but sin: not of fetching wood, or drawing water, if the time permit; not of cleaning your own shoes or your neighbour's.' This is the first recorded linking of sin with shoe-cleaning.

Hollywood spends much of its time and energy concentrating on the sins of the flesh, greed, lust, murder and theft.

Jung observed that 'all the old primitive sins are not dead, but are crouching in the dark corners of our modern hearts.'

And where sin crouches, be sure there will be a reporter from *The Sun* waiting to record it, photograph it and splash it all over the nation's breakfast tables.

Songs of Praise

Long-running BBC television programme which attracts vast audiences on Sunday evenings, visiting towns, cities and villages, meeting people, talking to them about their faith and playing their favourite hymns. While a new series is being recorded, the best of *Songs of Praise* is introduced, repeating highlights and much-requested hymns.

Songs of Praise is also the title of a hymn book, not now widely used.

SPIRE

William Golding once wrote a novel, called *The Spire*, about the erecting of such an edifice, which made it seem even more difficult than the building of the pyramids of Egypt. The principal character aspires to build the tallest spire of any cathedral in England, but by the time he has finished, many of the other characters have quietly, or not so quietly, expired. That spire was inspired by pride. The real symbolism of this arrowed construction atop the tower of a church is that it is reaching up closer towards God.

SUFFRAGAN BISHOP

'Suffragan' is the name given to an assistant bishop or bishops in an Anglican diocese. Sometimes misunderstandings can occur.

An example might be the following telephone conversation:

'Is that the Bishop of Bedford?'

'Yes . . .'

'Do you do pub lunches? May we book a table for four at 12.30, please?'

SUNDAY SCHOOL

A means of helping children to know about God and the Church.

Robert Raikes was 22 years old when he inherited *The Gloucester Journal* from his father in 1757. He had been educated at the Cathedral School and became concerned that children were growing up in ignorance of the Christian faith. In 1780, he hired four women to help establish a school which opened on weekdays and Sundays, where children could learn how to read and to learn Bible stories. Three years later he wrote about the development in his paper.

The article was not entitled *Raikes' Progress.* There was some opposition from people who thought no work of any kind should be done on Sundays, but the Sunday school was such a success that, before his death, Sunday schools had spread throughout the land.

Questions on the Bible in Sunday School have inspired many a memorable howler . . .

Teacher: 'Why didn't Jesus give in to the Devil's temptations?'
Child: ''Cos he didn't say ''please''!'

Teacher: 'Why cannot man live by bread alone?'
Child: 'Because he needs butter and jam as well.'

Surplice

This was once a white loose-fitting garment worn over fur coats in freezing churches. It has been in common use for around eight centuries. Worn by both Anglicans and Roman Catholics, whose version is called a cotta and is often lace fringed, surplices are subject to changing fashions, with hemlines going up and down like yoyos. Ecclesiastical outfitters have to make a living too!

A diverting account of the surplice's origin comes from Italy. A Roman Catholic priest, the future Saint Serge of Cramplinas, looked after two parishes on either side of a mountain. He discovered a way of sealing the sleeves and hemlines of his surplice and filling the garment with methane gas produced by his chickens. So, at one stroke, he became the first priest to fly – and discovered the answer to his parochial commuting problem.

Never one to inflict risks on others, he ascended on a trial flight over the Adriatic. Unfortunately, he forgot to take his lead ballast with him. Villagers at Grottamare saw the saint passing out to sea at a great height, the words of the *Nunc Dimittis* floating down from the sky. He was never seen again, and to this day the Feast of the Assumption or lift-off of St Serge is kept in remote Italian villages . . .

Swithin, St

A Bishop of Winchester in the ninth century.

When he died he asked to be buried 'where the sweet rain of heaven' could reach his grave – not in the Cathedral but out in the open, on the north or least-popular side of the churchyard. He wanted an ordinary simple grave, and was given what he wanted.

However, just over 100 years later, on 15 July, 964, his remains were 'translated' and re-buried in a beautiful shrine inside the Cathedral, because the people wished to honour him. And on the very day that this was done, it began to rain, and continued for 40 days. And so the superstition started that St Swithin had been so upset at having his body brought inside, that if ever it rained on 15 July in the future, it would rain for 40 days:

St Swithin's Day, if thou dost rain, for 40 days it will remain
St Swithin's Day, if thou be fair, for 40 days 'twill rain nae mair.

Synods

Contrary to popular belief, Jesus did not go around inveighing against 'publicans and synods' – although in the light of subsequent history, he could well have done. 'I hate, I despise your feast days and I will not smell in your solemn assemblies' says the Lord in the book of the prophet Amos.

Synods, in practical terms, are assemblies, particularly of bishops and other ecclesiastics. The word comes from the Greek *sunodos* and Latin, *synodus,* meaning 'meeting'.

Tabernacle

This was a portable shrine used by the Children of Israel during their wanderings in the desert before they were allowed into the Promised Land, Canaan. It was a structure of considerable complexity, as any portable church building would be.

In an inner chamber (the Holy of Holies) was the Ark of the Covenant containing the tablets of stone on which the Ten Commandments were engraved. In the outer chamber were the seven-branched lampstand, the incense altar and the table on which the shewbread was displayed. (The 'shewbread' is the 12 loaves of blessed, unleavened bread which ancient Hebrew priests placed every Sabbath in the sanctuary of the tabernacle. The Hebrews called it 'the bread of presence' – that is, the presence of God in the temple. In the 16th century, a German Bible translated this as 'Schaubrot' – and the word was promptly 'borrowed' into English as 'shewbread'.)

The whole tabernacle structure is described in infinite detail in the Book of Exodus.

At the Feast of Tabernacles, devout Jews build themselves shelters, which must be open to the sky so that they can be reminded of the time spent wandering in the desert. It's an early harvest festival, celebrating God's goodness, and, weather permitting, much time is spent in the booth or tabernacle.

Christians also have tabernacles, especially in Roman Catholic and High Anglican churches. The vessels containing the elements of bread and wine are kept safely in an ornamental container placed on the high altar. In some churches, the bread and wine are reserved in a container let into the wall of the sanctuary, and kept locked for safety.

Those who live in the Lord never see each other for the last time.

German proverb

Table of Kindred and Affinity

A table which is printed at the end of the Book of Common Prayer. For many centuries it provided intriguing and edifying reading for parishioners trapped in their pews for the duration of the sermon. It lists those people between whom marriage is forbidden.

A most entertaining list, amended in 1946, it included such prohibitions as 'A woman may not marry her father's mother's husband' or 'A man may not marry his wife's daughter's daughter.' It begins to look more ludicrous and crazy the longer one stares at it, and then like a film in the cinema, at the bottom of the page come the final closing words in big block capitals 'THE END'.

Many are those who on reading the list have prayed that the preacher, droning on in the background, might also come to his final closing words and that his sermon might at last also reach The End.

Televangelism

'Send us five dollars, and we'll pray for you.' In the United States, religious broadcasting is very big business indeed. Millions of dollars pour into the headquarters of the televangelists every week. They have to. Broadcasting coast-to-coast and across the world by satellite and cable links doesn't come cheap.

Religious broadcasting in this country has been 'regulated' since broadcasting began. In the United States, and increasingly around the world, the controls have been, or are being, removed. Those with the money can therefore directly evangelise their listeners and viewers, and appeal for money to further their work.

A number of those involved in televangelism have been involved in scandals and it remains to be seen what effect this will have on the phenomenal success and growth of the electronic church in America.

For far too long, the mainstream churches in this country have comforted each other, saying 'It couldn't happen here.' The signs are that it could, and that it will, as broadcasting becomes less and less regulated and more subject to market forces. Further, there are Christians, with the technology and the funding, ready and waiting to beam into your home via cable and satellite. The days of religious broadcasting as we know it in this country are numbered, make no mistake about that. 'Send us five quid and we'll pray for you.'

Ten Commandments

Moses comes down from the mountain after a hard day's bargaining with God. The people of Israel crowd round him to hear the latest position. Moses raises his arms; silence grips the crowd.

'My friends, there is good news and there is bad news. The good news is that we've got it down to just ten commandments. The bad news is that the seventh stays in.'

The seventh commandment is the one, above all others, that film-makers remember: 'Do not commit adultery.' Anyone would think there hadn't ever been any other commandments. Yet this one comes well down the list, after worshipping God and only God, not making graven images or idols, not taking God's name in vain, keeping the Sabbath, respecting parents and not murdering people. And, to complete the ten, do not steal, don't falsely accuse another, do not harbour jealousy for what other people have, their houses, their wives, slaves, cattle, donkeys or other possesions. The commandments are basic rules for keeping society sweet and well ordered – folk would be lost without them. So keep your thieving eyes off next door's donkey – and his wife!

Terce

One of the 'Little Hours' of the Divine Office, terce is a short, concise service appointed to be recited at the third hour (9 am). It is similar in structure to Sext and None, but it is less terse in Advent and Lent when other prayers are added.

Testament

'This is the last Will and Testament of Jeremiah Widget . . .' A testament is an agreement or covenant. The Old Testament is the collection of books which make up the larger part of the Bible, beginning with Genesis and ending with the book of the Prophet Malachi. The Old Testament is divided into three main types of writing: the books of the Law, the Prophets and the Writings which include the Psalms and Proverbs. The Old Testament is the Book of the Jewish faith, and Christians share this priceless treasure with the Jews. Old and New Testaments – the Bible – are a kind of last Will and Testament of God. Enquirers may learn something to their advantage when the will is opened and read.

Testimony

'There I was, on the number 49 bus, when suddenly I heard God say, "Marmaduke Molestranger, believe me, you will do great and wonderful things . . . and you can start by converting the heathen of Acacia Road." '

Testimony is a spoken or written witness to something that has happened. Within the New Testament, St Paul's account of what happened to him on the road to Damascus is an example of testimony: 'I was minding my own business on the road to Damascus when, all of a sudden, there was this blinding light shining on me. I was speechless. I fell to the ground and heard this voice saying, "Saul, Saul, why are you persecuting me?"

Since the days of the early Church, people have described their conversion to Christianity in similarly dramatic words. At mission meetings, new converts would often stand up and 'give their testimony' It was an example to others in the sense that, if it could happen to him or her, maybe it could happen to me, too, miserable sinner though I am.

Theology

The study of God. Once called the queen of sciences, it has since fallen from that pinnacle of acclaim.

Theology now ranks with sociology which, it is rumoured, is the study of those who don't need studying by those who do. Some of the blame for this decline must be laid at the door of theologians who, instead of wondering about God, argued about the number of angels who could stand shoulder to shoulder on the head of a pin. Even had this argument been concluded, it is far from clear how useful the information might have proved to be.

Today, theologians are recovering from a certain loss of nerve and

are again studying God – who, it is to be hoped, will both be flattered by their attentions and encouraged by their belief in His (or Her) existence.

TITHE

'To tithe' is to give a large chunk of your income in money or produce to the Church. It's a principle found in the Old Testament. Some Christians regularly hand over a tenth of their net earnings to the Church.

Within the Church of England, tithes used to be levied on the laity to maintain the clergy, help the poor, and assist the bishop. Then this system was abolished in favour of a tithe amounting to a tenth of all produce from the land. Some landowners bitterly resented this, and delayed payments for as long as they could. One farmer on his deathbed cursed the Church for stealing so much of his livelihood. Tithes were eventually abolished, but the principle remains.

TONGUES

'Speaking in tongues' occurs in the New Testament where St Paul declares that it was widespread at Corinth. However, he seems to have been highly suspicious of it, as no one (not even the person speaking) appears to have had the faintest idea what he or she was talking about.

In the 19th century, the condition was given the name *glossolalia* – which is not a word that trips easily off the tongue. In the 20th century speaking in tongues has grown in popularity in certain quarters, but in others *glossolalia* is simply considered a synonym for gibberish.

Tract

A tract is normally a region or area of land of indefinite extent, usually large. For example, people talk of 'vast tracts of desert', and a hymn includes the crazy line 'When I roar through tracts unknown'.

However, in religious circles, a tract is more often a treatise or discourse on a religious subject, which is usually short. The most famous English tracts were published in the 19th century and were known as Tracts for the Times. The people who wrote them were called Tractarians. They wrote in Oxford from 1833 – 41, and there were 90 tracts in all.

Nowadays, people in sandwich-boards, proclaiming the Wrath of God and the drawing nigh of the end of the world, quite often proffer tracts or pamphlets as they parade up and down the high street and through those endless tracts of desert described as shopping precincts, found in so many of our modern city-centres.

Trappists

Nothing to do with the von Trapp family and *The Sound of Music*, the Trappist are Cistercians who keep a strict rule of silence, spending about seven hours each day in worship.

Trappists, who take their name from the monastery of La Trappe, are vegetarians and devote themselves to farming and other manual work. They won't be found working in parishes, but that doesn't mean they're not working.

It's a bit like the vicar, really. Just because you can't spot him, it doesn't necessarily mean he's sitting in a deckchair watching Wimbledon on television.

Trinity

An exam paper on theological doctrine once included the question, 'Is the doctrine of the Trinity a comment on the family life of the Deity?' History does not record whether any student attempted an answer. The Trinity – Father, Son and Holy Spirit – remains a mystery.

A rabbi tells the story of a Jew who suddenly decided to cross the road, and launched himself into the path of a lorry. Unable to pull up, the lorry ran over him. The Jew lay dying in the road.

A priest rushed up and, kneeling down beside the Jew, said, 'Tell me, my son, do you believe in the Father, the Son and the Holy Spirit?'

The Jew looked up and with his last breath whispered, 'Here am I dying in the road and you're asking me riddles!'

Twelfth Night

The night of the day on which a certain lover received a large bird in a fruit tree and various other inappropriate and awkward gifts, including three French hens and two turtle doves.

It is on the twelfth day of Christmas – the feast of Epiphany, 6 January – that the Church remembers the coming of the Wise Men from the East (the ones who brought some rather extraordinary and awkward gifts for a baby in a stable).

Undertakers

Some time ago in one English city it was thought that funeral fees were getting too expensive. Undertakers were accused of taking their customers for a ride.

Uniformity

The different denominations within the Christian Church are working together for unity but not uniformity. This means that they will still continue to wear different uniforms, especially the Salvation Army.

For most churches, the clerical collar – or dog-collar – remains the most distinctive gear. Usually this has been worn with a black shirt for priests and purple for bishops, but in recent years grey and blue and even brown shirts have started to appear. These look not trendy but faintly ridiculous or even, in the case of brown, downright ugly!

Clergy also wear a cassock, surplice and vestments. Vestments include garments like the chasuble but not the vestibule, which (strange as it may seem) is not an undergarment worn by priests.

Urbi et Orbi

Solemn blessing given by the Pope to the city of Rome and the world, from the balcony in St Peter's Square, usually on Easter Day. This is probably the most televised blessing ever given. The Pope offers it in over 50 languages, thus ensuring that viewers around the world hear the blessing in their own tongue and making it worth the television coverage.

For reasons which remain obscure, the custom fell into disuse

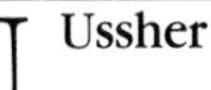

between 1870 and 1922, by which time the world really needed the Pope's blessing, and the pioneer of television, John Logie Baird, had been born and had started inventing.

USSHER

James Ussher, Archbishop of Armagh, lived from 1581 to 1656 and was appointed the first professor of divinity at Dublin at the age of 26.

One of his great triumphs was to calculate the exact date and time of creation, using the chronology in the Bible. The answer – 4004 BC at nine o'clock in the morning. Modern scientists believe him to have got the wrong answer. It's a shame that he is remembered chiefly for this mistake which, let's face it, anyone of us could have made in the 17th century.

So impressed was Oliver Cromwell with Ussher's holiness and scholarship, that he organised a state funeral for the Archbishop in Westminster Abbey.

VALENTINE, ST

The patron saint of greeting-card manufacturers. The original Valentine – martyred in third-century Italy – seems to have had no connection whatever with courting couples and doting newlyweds. The link seems to be the old, old belief that birds pair on 14 February – his Feast Day, beloved of lovers but not of postmen.

VATICAN

The Pope's smart address in Rome. Sited where Nero's Circus once stood, where the cries of Christian martyrs being torn to shreds by lions once echoed, the Vatican is its own state. With the Lateran Palace and the Pope's summer palace at Castelgandolfo, the Vatican was granted extra-territoriality in 1871. This takes some believing but the Vatican, though situated in Rome within the Italian capital, nonetheless is a sovereign state with its own diplomats, and its own Swiss guards. Its principal church is St Peter's – the largest church in Christendom, according to one source, 102 feet longer than St Paul's Cathedral in London.

The Vatican also contains the Sistine Chapel dating from the 15th century, adorned with the work of Michelangelo. To get the best view of his work, try lying on the floor and gazing at the ceiling.

Don't do this, however, if a new Pope is to be elected, or you may get trampled underfoot by cardinals from all over the world, who gather here to decide upon and elect the next occupant of the Throne of St Peter. The waiting world watches a chimney from which white smoke confirms a new pope's election, and black smoke, no decision. One year the waiting press corps were left in considerable doubt as grey smoke issued from the Sistine Chapel's chimney.

VENERABLE

Within the Roman Catholic Church, the title given to a dead person during the process of beatification, by which he or she may ultimately

be declared worthy of veneration. It's a word used to mark people who have led a holy and blameless life.

For some reason which is not too easy to determine, the word is also used to address live archdeacons within the Church of England. On the other hand, men who tour the diocese inspecting churchyards, swear in churchwardens and sit on committees without number deserve some respect. Nonetheless the temptation to substitute 'venomous' for 'venerable' is often irresistible.

Venerable Bede

Not the most ancient part of a necklace, but a monk from ancient days in England. Bede was a monk from Jarrow who wrote a *History of the English Church and People.*

Although the authors of *1066 and All That* constantly refer to him as 'The Venomous Bede', a classic schoolboy howler, he was a man of singular gentleness, holiness and scholarship, who entered Jarrow monastery at the age of eight and didn't leave it until his death.

He was buried in Durham Cathedral, where the Latin couplet inscribed on his shrine possibly gave rise to his 'title' and to its subsequent use in the Christian church: *Haec sunt in fossa/Bedae venerabilis ossa* (Here in the grave are the bones of the venerable – i.e. worthy – Bede).

Verger

Verger, or more correctly 'Virger' as at Canterbury Cathedral and St Albans Abbey, is the title of one of a cathedral's most important officers. He is the official who carries the 'verge' (Latin *virga*) or staff of office before a dignitary and walks at the head of procession.

Vergers are responsible, like sacristans, for the care of the building and the sacred vessels and the lighting of lamps. Most vergers are wise.

Vespers

An evening service, part of the monastic cycle of prayer.

The service of Evensong in the Book of Common Prayer is in part modelled on Vespers. Some of the most glorious music to be heard is that written by Monteverdi for this service.

Vespers is not always a glorious occasion, however. The Sicilian Vespers is the name given to the massacre of between three and four thousand French in Sicily on 30 March, 1282, for which the starting signal was the tolling of the bell summoning the faithful to Vespers. Seemingly innocent things, like a church bell tolling, are not always what they seem to be!

Vestments

Clothes worn by clergy taking services, these date from between the fourth and ninth centuries, and were the original 'Sunday Best'. Within the Roman Catholic Church, their use is closely regulated. In the 16th century clerical attire became a matter of fierce controversy and several London clergy were sacked for refusing to wear a surplice as required

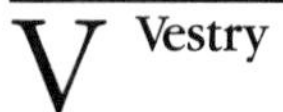

by Matthew Parker, Elizabeth I's Archbishop of Canterbury (the original 'Nosey Parker', who enquired too closely for comfort into the conduct of the clergy and ecclesiastical affairs generally). Vestments were held by the Puritans to smack of 'Popery'.

Though clergy rarely lose their jobs today because of what they wear, one priest nearly lost his nerve when, putting on the vestments for the 8 o'clock communion service, he became trapped in a long white flowing garment called an alb.

What should he do? If he dashed into the church with muffled cries for help, the few in the congregation might have run from the building shouting, 'Ghosts!'

Wrestling mightily, the priest freed himself from the alb's coils and recovered sufficiently to take the service. Given the dangers of vestments, many parishes when advertising for a priest specify whether or not they expect the applicant to wear them in church.

VESTRY

A room attached to the church were the vestments are kept.

On 2 November, 1985, there was a great Service of Thanksgiving in St Albans Abbey to mark the completion of the Abbey Appeal for the new Chapter House. The congregation waited and waited for the service to begin. But begin it could not, because the Bishop of St Albans and the Bishop of Hertford, the Dean of St Albans and the Archdeacon, the Diocesan Director of Ordinands (DDO) and the Bishop's Chaplain were all upstairs in the vestry, and the door to the vestry had jammed. There they were, six helpless and hapless clergy with one of the Cathedral servers, and there were they stuck. The vestry has a balcony and so for fifteen minutes they remained peering down over the balcony on to the uplifted anxious faces and the hard stone floor below, while the Precentor proclaimed their predicament to the chortling congregation.

When a verger kindly enquired whether they wanted a ladder, the Bishop's Chaplain emphatically responded 'No', while, to his horror, the DDO, intrepid and rash, equally definitely answered 'Yes'. A ladder was therefore produced, and up it climbed an architect and a brave churchwarden, brandishing tools with which they then struggled vigorously but in vain to prise open the offending door.

Meanwhile, the DDO, yet more intrepid and rash, seized another implement in his hand (a screwdriver or spanner or some such weapon), and began to attack a part of the wall, crying aloud, 'If I can cut through here, down a ladder let us go.' The Bishop of St Albans and he, being accustomed to scrambling over pinnacles of mountains in search of birds, thought nothing of such a perilous descent; but for the Bishop's Chaplain quite the most dreadful part of the ordeal was the appalling prospect of having to negotiate this ghastly swaying ladder with or without gaily flowing robes.

So there the Chaplain stood, praying like mad that the architect would succeed in opening the door before the valiant DDO could cut through his wretched wall. 'I am almost there!' shouted he, to the

Chaplain's unutterable dismay – but to the obvious delight of the Bishop of St Albans who was happily on the verge of clambering down in full episcopal splendour. The Bishop's Chaplain's heart sank to his boots but then suddenly, Hallelujah, his prayers were answered. The architect and the warden succeeded, and behold, the door was open. Through it they all passed, down the stairs they strode, and the service at last began, to rapturous applause.

VICAR

In the olden days when the bishop appointed a priest to have the cure of souls in a parish he was known as the rector (or ruler). However, some parishes were in the care of the local monastery, and the abbot was therefore the rector. It then became necessary for him to appoint a vice-rector, or deputy, to look after the parish on his behalf, and this vice-rector became known as the vicar. Nowadays, the names 'rector' and 'vicar' mean the same; some parishes traditionally have one, and some the other.

There are, of course, some vicars who are even now no strangers to vice. And some rectors too, But they remain very much the exception, although greatly loved by the popular press.

Vicars are normally portrayed on stage and screen as half-wits, fools, simpletons, imbeciles and idiots. They are sometimes like this in real life too. However, when a parish is about to receive a new one, the churchwardens usually write to the bishop asking for a man with all the qualities of the Archangel Gabriel who must be in his forties, and married with at least two children.

If a vicar travels by train wearing his dog-collar he can be sure of having the compartment to himself. He can indeed make certain of this by smiling at people out of the window when the train stops at a station and beckoning to them to come to join him. If that fails and they still persist in entering, he needs only to toss a hymn-book in their direction and loudly announce some number to have them fleeing in panic to the other end of the train.

That clergyman soon becomes an object of contempt who, being often asked out to dinner, never refuses to go.

St Jerome

Vicar's Wife

One day a vicar and his wife were about to set off on their holiday.

'Please don't pack your dog-collar,' said the wife. 'I'm so tired of people, year after year, always knowing that you're a vicar even when we're away on our holiday.'

'All right,' he replied. And he didn't take it.

On their first evening at the hotel they had to share a table in the dining-room with a young couple.

'Excuse me,' said the young man, 'I hope you don't mind my asking, but aren't you a vicar?'

'Well, yes,' replied the cleric. 'But how on earth did you know?'

'Well, sir,' said the man. 'Your wife looks such a typical vicar's wife.'

Video

In the old days, people took a nostalgic walk through wedding pictures. Now it's more likely to be a long look at the whole day, from the moment the bride-to-be totters down to breakfast and wonders whether to laugh or cry at the thought of marrying Wayne (or is it Darren?) to the last look at the honeymoon car daubed with lipstick and a rattle of empty tins tied to the back bumper. And there will be all the scenes in between – the wait for the flowers to arrive, the hole in the bridesmaid's tights, the rush back to the shoe shop to get the pageboy's size right this time. Then there's the panic over the wedding cars when the garage rings up and asks 'One limo or two?'

At the church, the vicar is asked to stand so that his gleaming white surplice doesn't confuse the automatic aperture control on the video camera. Then it's 'Could you speak up, Vic? We can't quite hear you on the sound channel from the back of the church . . . yes, that's better.' And why did the cassette run out just as they made their vows? The verger had to be slipped an extra fiver for promising not to sing, or rather growl, too near the microphone . . . and there was all that fuss

over whether we had copyright permission to record *You'll never walk alone* as the bride walked up the aisle.

Maybe we should have stuck to good old still photography, and left it to a professional at that, eh, Dad?

VIRGIN

Difficult word this, with so many meanings.

The Virgin Mary, mother of Jesus, inspiring devotion among countless millions of Christians.

Virgin, purveyors of countless millions of records, inspiring devotion among young people, and deafness among their parents and neighbours.

Then there are those Foolish Virgins who forget to call at the ironmonger's for some paraffin or oil for their lamps on their way to a Jewish wedding likely to last three days. At lighting-up time the silly girls find they're fresh out of oil and appeal to wiser ladies of the lamp, who refuse to help. They have since inspired countless oaths denoting lack of devotion accompanied by great feelings of angst.

VISITATION

After Mary had said 'Fiat mihi secundum verbum tuum' which means 'be it unto me according to thy words' to the Angel Gabriel who had come to announce the coming birth of Jesus, she went to visit her cousin Elizabeth. This was called The Visitation.

The answer to the question, 'Why did Mary walk to see Elizabeth?' is 'Because the Angel had taken her Fiat.'

WAKE

In Ireland this is a vigil (or keeping awake) and feast at a funeral. So much noise is made at a wake – singing, shouting jokes, telling stories – that there is little or no chance of anyone falling asleep. Indeed, on one or two occasions the noise has been thought fit to wake the dead, which would be very embarrassing and a cause of scandal, not to mention a reason to call a halt to the wake.

In England, the word meant an all-night vigil before certain holy days or feasts. It dates from Anglo Saxon times. Eventually it came to mean the fair held to mark a festival, hence the Wakes Weeks, found in the north of England.

He who is near the church is often far from God.

French proverb

WARDENS

There are two types of churchwarden (the correct name for warden). One is an old-fashioned long, clay pipe. The other is a lay official elected by parishioners.

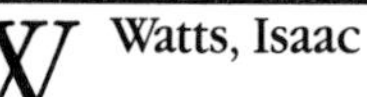

When the bishop comes to a parish church the wardens march in front of him, bearing their official wands or sticks, presumably to beat a path to his seat through the midst of the congregation.

Watts, Isaac

Born in Southampton, Watts is recognised as one of the greatest of all English hymn-writers and, like Charles Wesley, was a Free Churchman. Watts was the author of *When I survey the wondrous Cross,* which Wesley described as 'the greatest hymn in the English language'. Wesley himself was no mean hymn-smith and wrote some 5,500 hymns, including *Hark! The Herald Angels Sing* and *Love Divine.*

Isaac Watts also wrote some of the very best-known hymns including *Jesus shall reign where'er the sun,* and *O God our help in Ages Past.*

Wee Frees

A minority of members of the Free Church of Scotland who, rather than join with the United Presbyterian Church to form the United Free Church in 1900, stayed out in the cold and were thus called the Wee Frees.

Whitsun

Another name for Pentecost, 50 days after Easter when the Holy Spirit descended upon the Apostles in the guise of a rushing, mighty wind and tongues of flame. In their excitement they all started speaking at once and using the most extraordinary language. Everyone was naturally amazed, as they were not accustomed to hearing such language emerging from the lips of Apostles.

'Whit' comes from the word 'white', and so naturally on Whit Sunday the Church, with its love of the unexpected, dresses its priests and ministers and adorns the altar in red. Whitsun brides, however, still seem to prefer white to red, for Whitsun is a popular season for weddings. Philip Larkin wrote a poem about this called, reasonably enough, *The Whitsun Weddings.*

Traditionally it has also been a favourite time for baptisms with long white christening robes.

At one time Whit Monday was kept as a Bank Holiday but nowadays, although there are two Bank Holiday Mondays in the month of May, neither of them is by any means necessarily at Whitsuntide.

Widow's Mite

When rich people were throwing money into a collecting box, in the New Testament story, this poor widow threw in all she had, which happened to be a mite. Poor wee mite.

Actually a mite was the smallest coin of the currency of the time, a sort of Palestinian farthing. Jesus witnessed this particular incident – and said the good woman had given more than the rich, because what they gave they could easily afford, but she gave her all. Now there's a moral!

Wise Men

Nowhere does the Bible actually say there were three. It simply mentions three gifts. And nowhere does it say they were kings. Nowadays, they would probably hail a taxi and cry, 'Follow that star!'

Woodforde, The Revd. James

Eighteenth-century country parson who kept a diary every day from the age of 18 until just before his death whose diaries are still a popular record of eighteenth-century English country life. He spent the greater part of his life at Weston Longville in Norfolk, and loved enormous meals and gossip.

Wren

In this context, this is neither a bird nor a member of the Women's Royal Navy, but Sir Christopher Wren, the architect of St Paul's Cathedral.

If a well-known verse is anything to go by, the project offered him an excuse to avoid unwelcome contact:

Sir Christopher Wren
Went out to dine with some men.
He said, 'If anyone calls,
Tell them I'm designing St Paul's.

In the Great Fire of London, 89 churches and old St Paul's had been lost, and it was Wren who magnificently resurrected them even more splendidly than before. In addition to St Paul's (his great masterpiece), his other works include St Mary-le-Bow, St Clement Danes (as in oranges and lemons, say the bells of) and St Bride's, Fleet Street.

Wren died on 16 February 1723 and lies buried beneath his own great monument – the inscription at the entrance to the choir reads in Latin: 'If you seek his monument, look around.'

Xavier, St Francis

How nice to have a name beginning with 'X'. Very useful for signing cheques like Annie Oakley's uncle down in Texas.

Francis X was born in Navarre in the 16th century, and ordained priest in Venice in 1537. He travelled vast distances as a missionary to the East Indies and to Japan, and is said to have converted 700,000 people – astonishing, considering he suffered habitually from seasickness and just couldn't get his tongue efficiently round foreign languages.

YAHWEH

The old name for God, pronounced 'yar way' and meaning the same as Jehovah.

'Yar way' sounds very much like the aggressive cry of a band of raucous football supporters, while 'Jehovah' is much more like the 'heave ho' of the Volga boatmen.

A story is told of a drunken rabbi who was heard rolling home at the end of the Sabbath day singing, 'I did it Yaweh.'

YORK

After centuries of controversy between York and Canterbury, Pope Innocent VI in the 16th century put an end to any further quarrelling and monkey-business by making the Archbishop of York 'Primate of England'. The Archbishop of Canterbury, however, was given precedence with the title 'Primate of All England', and that made *all* the difference.

York Minster was struck by lightning in 1984 after the consecration of the present Bishop of Durham. Nothing to do with the good Bishop, and nothing to do with God. Lightning strikes where it will, and the Minster just happened to be in the way.

A bishop should die preaching.
John Jewel

YOUNG WIVES' GROUP

Less-senior branch of Mothers' Union – otherwise known as Young Mothers.

Notice in Vancouver Parish Magazine:

'There will be a meeting of Young Mothers on Tuesday. All those wishing to become Young Mothers are invited to meet the vicar in the Vestry.'

YULE

A word meaning 'noise' or 'clamour' which used to be applied to Christmas, which certainly remains a time of noise and clamour in the high street today.

The name seems to have virtually disappeared, but in the days of wood and coal fires the yule log played an important part in the Christmas festivities. Indeed, the bringing in of the yule log on Christmas Eve used to be an elaborate ceremony. Preferably, this log had to be big enough to burn in the hearth right through from Christmas Eve to Twelfth Night. However, if the hearth was not big enough, it ought at least to burn through to Christmas Day.

ZACCHAEUS

The New Testament loves people whose names begin with Z. Zacchaeus, pronounced 'Zack key us', is one of the New Testament's minor characters. A small man with a big job (he was a filthy-rich tax collector and consequently hated by all) he climbed a tree because he could not see over the heads of the crowd to get a view of Jesus. The tree was a sycamore, and Zacchaeus could then see a bit more. Jesus saw him too, called him down, and invited Himself to stay at Zacc's for the night.

ZACHARIAS

Zacharias, pronounced 'Zacka rye us,' appears in the Gospels as he was father of John the Baptist.

He was already an old man when he learnt that his wife Elizabeth was to bear a son. This announcement rendered him speechless with amazement. In fact, he was so shocked that he lost his voice and became quite dumb. This was a trifle unfortunate as he was in the midst of some ceremony in the Temple at the time, and the congregation were waiting for him to continue.

His voice remained lost for some considerable period, and until he found it he was forced to resort to writing notes. When the baby was eventually born and the time came for him to be named, the people naturally assumed that he would be named Zacharias after his father; but no. Zacharias asked (says the King James version of the Bible) for a writing table, and to their consternation wrote 'His name is John.'

Ever since then John has been one of the most popular names for boys, and Zacharias one of the least. Although in recent years Zack and Zak have started to make a come-back.

Zebedee

A name well-known to children in the 1960s as the companion of Dougal and Florence, but also in the Gospels the father of the disciples James and John. They left him in a boat and went off to follow Jesus. He was never heard of again until he sprang onto the screen as the magic roundabout revolved to announce that it was time for bed.

Zion

Spelt sometimes with a 'Z' and sometimes with an 'S', this is God's holy hill or mount at Jerusalem. It is also a popular name for nonconformist chapels, especially in Wales, similar to Beulah (after the black American actress Beulah Bondi who slaved away in the kitchen in so many Hollywood films), Ebenezer (after E. Scrooge, the famous lover of Christmas) and Salem (of Witches fame). Salem of course is really Jerusalem where Mount Zion stands, and this Zion or Sion itself sometimes stands for the city as in the hymn –

Glorious things of thee are spoken
Sion, city of our God.

That same hymn also goes on to talk of the

Solid joys and lasting treasure
None but Sion's children know.

These solid joys are thought perhaps to refer to the rather stodgy suet puddings which some children knew well in their nursery days in days of old.

A typical Welsh chapel might be named the Ebenezer Baptist Salem Beulah Pentecostal Harry Secombe Sion Church of God.

Give me one hundred preachers who fear nothing but sin and desire nothing but God, and I care not a straw whether they be clergymen or laymen, such alone will shake the gates of hell and set up the Kingdom of God upon earth.

John Wesley